One Great Ground of Hope

ONE GREAT

GROUND OF HOPE

Christian Missions and Christian Unity

BY HENRY P. VAN DUSEN

THE WESTMINSTER PRESS · *Philadelphia*

Library of Congress Catalog Card No. 61–8496

To my Colleagues

of the Joint Committee

of the International Missionary Council

and the World Council of Churches

Contents

As though in preparation for such a time as this, God has been building up a Christian fellowship which now extends into almost every nation, and binds citizens of them all together in true unity and mutual love. No human agency has planned this. It is the result of the great missionary enterprise of the last hundred and fifty years. . . . Almost incidentally the great world fellowship has arisen; it is the great new fact of our era. . . .

Here is one great ground of hope for the coming days—this world-wide Christian fellowship, this ecumenical movement. . . .

It is of urgent importance that we become aware of it, that we further it in every way open to us, and that through it we take our part in providing for the Spirit of Christ the agency by which he may transform the world.

—WILLIAM TEMPLE, in
The Church Looks Forward, PP. 2–4.

PREFACE

Some of the material in this small book was initially prepared as the Powell Lectures delivered at the Canadian School of Missions in Toronto in November, 1952. Excerpts from a later draft constituted part of the Otis Memorial Lectures at Wheaton College, Norton, Massachusetts, in March, 1960. I am indebted to these two institutions for gracious hospitality and encouragement on the occasions of the delivery of the lectures, and I am especially grateful to President A. Howard Meneely for waiving Wheaton's rights to publication. The early pages retraverse some of the territory explored in my *World Christianity: Yesterday, Today, and Tomorrow*, pp. 35–39, now out of print. I have not hesitated to reproduce certain statements from that earlier discussion.

During the past eight years, the manuscript has been frequently recast and revised, as indeed was mandatory since the story that the book seeks to set forth was changing from month to month. The aim has been to trace the major aspects of the development to the end of 1960.

A number of friends and co-workers have given prodigal assistance.

Two of my close associates have examined the final draft in its entirety. Dr. Frank W. Price, Director of the Missionary Research Library and Adjunct Professor in Union Seminary, has lent the invaluable resource of his unequaled knowledge by scrutinizing every statement as to its factual accuracy and sound interpretation and has thus saved the manuscript from many errors, although I have not followed his wise judgment in every particular. Dr. Norman Goodall, my colleague in the work of the Joint Committee of the International Missionary Council and the World Council of Churches, has made a number of perceptive comments and suggestions; and I have profited by a prepublication reading of his book *The Ecumenical Movement*, which is to be issued in 1961 and which admirably complements this volume at many points.

9

The "Chronology of Christian Unity: 1795–1960" has been prepared by Miss Barbara Griffis, librarian of the William Adams Brown Ecumenical Library at Union Theological Seminary, with the help of my research assistant, Mr. James W. Bergland. No effort has been spared to make this "Chronology" both complete and accurate, although judgment will necessarily vary as to what should be included or omitted in so comprehensive a listing.

Lastly, as with earlier books, I would pay special and grateful tribute to a corps of competent and devoted secretaries who have copied and recopied the material in successive versions, especially to Miss Gladys Burkhart, who was largely responsible for the penultimate draft, and to Mrs. Alice C. Strobel, Miss Rae Beth Parrott, and Mrs. Virginia Douglas, who have completed the final manuscript and assisted in the preparation of the index.

H.P.V.D.

Union Theological Seminary
New York, N.Y.
April 27, 1961

Introduction

Among contemporary Christian historians, three generalizations have been so frequently advanced, so plentifully documented, and so widely recognized that they may be said to have won an almost universal acceptance. They may be described as historic axioms.

1

By any reasonable calculus that might be proposed, the period of which we are immediate heirs—roughly the last one hundred and fifty years from the dawn of the nineteenth century to midpoint in the twentieth—was the epoch of largest, most varied, and most notable Christian achievement in the nearly two millenniums of Christian history.

To many, that statement may come as a startling surprise. Those of us who live under the shadow of recent events always lack perspective rightly to appraise their significance. Moreover, it is the habit of youth—and we are still a youthful nation—to disparage its parentage and to idealize its remoter ancestry. So, in the life of the church, there is always the cry: Back to the fathers! to the Middle Ages! to the Reformation! to the early church! But future generations looking back in a perspective that is not ours are likely to take for granted that the last century and a half stands forth as the period of greatest Christian advance in the nearly two thousand years since Christianity's beginning.

In terms of *geographic outreach*, the rapidly multiplying agencies of the Christian mission carried their gospel to the utmost circumference of human habitation, to peoples and areas and even continents previously untouched by Christian influence. Only one who has been at pains to examine the facts with some care can appreciate at their full the sweep and reach and depth of that penetration. It can be grasped most readily by a simple comparison of two world maps indicating the limits of the church's outmost boundaries at the beginning and at the close of the period. It is vividly symbolized in the fact that our most authoritative *History of the Expansion of Christianity*[1] finds it necessary to devote as much space to set forth that expansion during the nineteenth century as had been required for the whole of the preceding eighteen centuries.

In terms of *numerical growth,* during the same period the Christian churches multiplied their memberships manifold, fully as rapidly as the corresponding increases in populations. Today approximately one third of the earth's populace is, at least professedly, Christian.

History knows no parallel to that accomplishment. No other movement of any kind has ever spread so rapidly or so widely, or has ever won so many persons of so many races and cultures to its adherence in a comparable span of time. No other allegiance has ever held so many or so large a proportion of mankind in its support. The upshot has been summarized thus:

> Today in all the representative regions of the globe and in every land save three . . . there are organized Christian churches. For the first time in Christian history the church has become ecumenical in the literal meaning of that word. Its boundaries are coextensive with the inhabited globe.[2]

In our day, for the first time Christianity has become a world faith.

At the same time, in terms of *influence upon the common life of humanity,* Christian ideals and the labors of Christians effected greater emancipations, reforms, and improvements in the lot of all sorts and conditions of men than had ever before been wrought by any single influence in any previous comparable epoch.

Wherever the church carried its evangel of spiritual liberation and redemption it bore also the intrinsic Christian concern for healing of body, enlightenment of mind, elevation of the circumstances of life; and it established the practical instrumentalities—

---

[1] K. S. Latourette, *A History of the Expansion of Christianity,* 7 vols. Harper & Brothers, 1937–1945.

[2] John A. Mackay in the *International Review of Missions* (October, 1948).

hospitals and leprosariums, schools and colleges, printing presses and publishing houses, agricultural institutes and social agencies, etc.—to give that concern concrete effect.

Moreover, to the secular historian, the nineteenth century was the "century of reform." It was marked by a sequence of movements in furtherance of human welfare, beginning early in the century with agitation for the abolition of the slave trade, then for prison reform, for improvement in the working conditions of women and children, for the extension of medicine and public health, for emancipation from chattel slavery, for the elimination of child labor, for the organization and recognition of labor, for equality of the sexes, for temperance, for slum clearance, for world peace. Each of these efforts, at its inception, was a difficult and daring crusade against then-prevailing practices and prejudices. Virtually every one of them, with the single but humbling exception of labor organization, was prompted by Christian indignation, inspired by Christian vision, and pioneered by men and women of profound Christian conviction and consecration.[3]

These are among the facts that validate Dr. Kenneth Scott Latourette's well-known characterization of the nineteenth century as "The Great Century"—the greatest in the history of Christianity or of any other movement.

Those who are entrusted with the destiny of Christianity in our day and those who essay to forecast its prospects for the days ahead need to be laid hold of by this unchallengeable fact: they are heirs and trustees of the mightiest accomplishments for human welfare and of the most notable fulfillments of Christian duty that have ever been entrusted to a single generation.

2

The greatness of this legacy of Christian achievement is twofold.

During the past century and a half, the life of the non-Roman[4]

---

[3] Compare Hugh Martin, ed., *Christian Social Reformers of the Nineteenth Century.* Student Christian Movement, 1927. All this was truer in Anglo-Saxon lands than elsewhere. And of course a complete account of social reform in the nineteenth century, especially toward the close, would need to give large attention to Marxism.

[4] The qualifying phrase "non-Roman" should be inserted in most of the generalization that follows. To avoid tiresome reiteration, the qualification is usually omitted, but it should be constantly borne in mind. Little of what is said in these chapters embraces the Roman Catholic Church.

Christian churches of the world has been marked by two major developments, each of unprecedented proportions and power in the history of Christendom. It is these two developments together which constitute the most significant feature of Christianity in the modern era and give to this period of a century and a half a character as distinctive and as distinguished as any previous "Great Age" of Christian faith—the early church, the Middle Ages, the Protestant Reformation. One is the modern *movement of Christian missions;* the other, the contemporary *movement for Christian unity.*

In their inner character and impulsions, these two historic developments—*Christian missions* and *Christian unity*—appear sharply contrasted, indeed almost antithetic. *One* has been a movement of expansion, of extension. Its impulses were centrifugal. To use a familiar psychological term, its mood was extrovert. It pressed outward across the earth and into secular society as Christians faced with new insight and recognition of responsibility the unredeemed areas and needs of their world. The *other* has been a movement of consolidation, of unification. Its impulses were centripetal, its mood introvert. It turned the attention of church leaders inward upon themselves as they faced up with new honesty to the unchristian scandal of their own divisions. *One* aimed to extend the reach of Christian influence and Christian allegiance to the uttermost parts of the world and into the most neglected aspects of the common life so that Christianity might become in fact what it had always been in ideal and had never been in fact—a world religion. The *other* sought to bridge the chasms and level the barriers that separate Christians into denominations and sects so that the Christian church might begin to become in truth what it had always been in profession and has never been in reality, a single organism worthy of its own self-designation as the "body of Christ."

Despite this contrast in perspective and purpose, the two movements have been intimately related. To a marked degree, both sprang from the same source—a third historic development more basic and creative than either Christian missions or Christian unity—a remarkable series of *spiritual renewals* flowing from the Evangelical Revival, the Wesleys and Whitefield, Finney and Moody and Drummond. Previously, religious revival had usually parented Christian schism; but, as Dr. Latourette has pointed out, "The religious awakenings of the eighteenth and nineteenth

centuries have been among the most potent sources of the growing movement toward Christian unity."[5] Moreover, despite their
differences in mood and objectives, the two movements were
driven by similar compulsions, especially a greatly quickened
awareness of obligation to fulfill Christ's hope "that they all may
be one . . . that the world may believe." In considerable measure,
they pressed forward under identical leadership.

It is these two developments together in their present-day expression which constitute the contemporary reality of ecumenical
Christianity. Indeed, the two together are being increasingly re-
ferred to as the "Ecumenical Reformation," a reformation in the
twentieth century as radical and perhaps ultimately as far-reaching as the Protestant Reformation of the sixteenth century. This
view of its significance is held not merely by enthusiasts for the
movement or by Protestants and Orthodox only. Perhaps the
best-informed Roman Catholic scholar has expressed a similar
judgment: " 'The ecumenical movement' has brought changes in
religious thinking comparable to the changes caused by the Reformation of the sixteenth century."[6] This fact was given classic
definition by the youthful Secretary of the American Interseminary Movement, now an Associate General Secretary of the
World Council of Churches: "It is a reformation which amid the
provincialism of the churches asserts the world mission of the
church. It is a reformation which amid the disunity of the
churches asserts the unity of the church."[7]

3

Although each of these historic developments had its origin at
about the same time, the dawn of the nineteenth century, and
although they advanced side by side and in close contact through
the last one hundred and fifty years, their relationships have *not*

[5] Unpublished manuscript: "Divisive and Unifying Tendencies in Revival
Movements."

[6] Bernard Leeming, S.J., *The Churches and the Church* (The Newman
Press, 1960), p. vii. In support of this high estimate of the historic significance
of the ecumenical development, Father Leeming quotes a fellow Catholic:
"Père Boyer speaks soberly when he says: 'There may be different opinions
about the excellence of the World Council; but it must be recognized and all
Catholics ought to realize that with it a new force has arisen and it would
be unwise not to take account of it.' " *Gregorianum*, Vol. XXXV (1954), p. 593.
Quoted in *op. cit.*, p. ix.

[7] Robert S. Bilheimer, *What Must the Churches Do?* (Harper & Brothers,
1947), p. 80.

been strictly reciprocal. On the contrary, causative influences
have moved preponderantly from the first to the second. *The
Christian world mission has been the principal parent of the
effort after Christian unity.*

The contemporary movement for Christian unity is by no
means a simple phenomenon, springing from a single origin, and
moving along a direct line of advance. On the contrary, it is a
bafflingly intricate network of many different and sometimes
seemingly contradictory endeavors. In our incurable fondness for
clear patterns and neat explanations, we would prefer to suppose
that, somewhere, somehow, at a particular moment of history and
at one place, the minds of Christians or their leaders were
gripped by the realization that the church of Christ *should* be
one, and that forthwith, the modern movement for Christian
unity came to birth. Actually, history shows a very different record. Over a period of about a century and a half in a variety of
places and circumstances and under numerous and different
forms, impulses to reach across historic Christian divisions, and
conviction of the obligation to do so, became manifest. There is
no more impressive evidence of the determinative working of the
living Spirit of God in this matter than just the *multiplicity* and
diversity of origins of what we have now learned to recognize as
a single development and to identify as *the* movement for Christian unity.

Is there, then, no common pattern that can be discerned among
these many and contrasted events? Yes, there is one. Through all
the multitudinous, multiform, and variegated items, there is a
single common thread: at virtually every point *the conviction
and impulses of Christian unity originated within the enterprise
of Christian missions.*

It was a common sense of obligation for a more vigorous and
effective fulfillment of common missionary responsibilities that
first prompted individual Christians of diverse traditions to trans-
cend historic barriers and come together for consultation, then
common planning, and finally united action. It has been the requirements of their missionary programs that have led churches
into most forms of interdenominational collaboration. From the
directors of these programs on the mission field—first, missionaries, and latterly, the leaders of the younger churches—has come
the most urgent insistence upon larger and speedier Christian

unity both in the parent churches of the West and in their youthful children across the world.

It was on the mission field, in India, that representatives of five different Protestant communions first joined forces to sponsor a specific interdenominational project.[8] It was to plan and to man missionary tasks more adequately that the first important transdenominational conferences were held. It was altogether appropriate, indeed inevitable, that the first great world-wide interdenominational conclave of this century should have been a missionary convention—at Edinburgh in 1910. And that from it as a germinative seed plot should have sprung, directly or indirectly, the major world movements for Christian co-operation, e.g., both of the immediate parents of the World Council of Churches—the World Conference on Faith and Order and the Universal Christian Council for Life and Work—as well as the International Missionary Council.

Moreover, it is on the mission field and among the younger Christian churches, richest fruitage of missionary outreach, that concrete achievement in almost every type and phase of Christian unity has come earliest, has moved fastest, and has gone farthest. We repeat: *the Christian world mission has been both the precursor and the progenitor of the effort after Christian unity.* This fact furnishes the major thesis of this book. The detailed historical exposition will occupy us in Part I.

[8] The Zenana Bible and Medical Mission. See Part I, p. 42.

Yesterday:

A Century and a Half of Christian Unity

I

We have said: the movement for Christian unity has found manifold forms of expression. To be sure, all proceeded from a single impulse and resolve—to join inadequate resources for a more worthy witness and a more effective program, to overpass traditional barriers and long-accepted chasms between Christians, to approximate more nearly that wholeness of the body of Christ to which all Christians have always been, in principle, committed. But to the uninitiated, the varieties and complexities of this development are a source of confusion and bafflement.[1] To the discerning historian, they are clear evidence of its spontaneity, scope, and strength. Only an informed and disciplined exercise of imagination can lead one into a realization of either the novelty or the magnitude of the achievement. We may be aided in this effort after comprehension by two historic contrasts. One concerns *church union,* the other *co-operation.*

1. During the first eighteen centuries of Christian history, despite unceasing prayer for the unity of Christ's church, much talk and no little conference, scarcely a single important achievement of church union was recorded.[2] On the contrary, almost every one of the eighteen centuries witnessed at least one new major, permanent schism; since the Protestant Reformation, divisions within the church have multiplied to the present appalling total

[1] Canon Iremonger, biographer of the late Archbishop William Temple, speaks of the "almost countless organizations, societies, and conferences" making it difficult "even for those most familiar with the ramifications to avoid being lost in a tangle of parallel organizations." F. A. Iremonger, *William Temple, Archbishop of Canterbury, His Life and Letters* (Oxford University Press, 1948), p. 389. Quoted by Bernard Leeming, *op. cit.,* p. vii. Father Leeming, an extraordinarily well-informed Roman Catholic interpreter, adds that this complex of organizations "seems almost like a forest primeval."

[2] The only notable instance was the reunion of the greater part of Western Christendom, following the "papal schism," at the Council of Constance in 1415.

of more than three hundred.[3] For eighteen hundred years, the practice of Christians with respect to the unity of Christ's church precisely contradicted their professions. In contrast, while the past one hundred and fifty years have seen the coming to birth of a number of new Christian sects, they have also recorded a steady succession of actual church unions, totaling over a hundred. Some of these have taken the form of *re*unions within great denominational families—Methodist, Presbyterian, Lutheran, etc. But a steadily increasing proportion of consummated unions have brought together churches of diverse and sometimes sharply contrasted communions, as in the United Church of Canada and United Churches in South India, Japan, China, North India, the Philippines, and the United States. Here, again, history knows no parallel or precedent in the previous Christian centuries. In these latter years, Christian action in the matter of church union has begun to accord with Christian profession.

2. The second contrast is this: Up to the dawn of the nineteenth century, so far as our records show, there was scarcely an organization or fellowship of any kind, whether in a local community or in a nation, through which churches or even individual Christians of different denominational affiliations came together to confer regarding their respective Christian tasks, let alone to plan and work together in the discharge of common Christian responsibilities. Today, a century and a half later, there are thousands of interdenominational bodies. They range from councils or federations of churches in countless towns and cities (nearly a thousand in the United States alone and some two hundred in Great Britain), through national councils of churches in almost every country on all continents where diverse Christian communions are found in any considerable variety and strength, supplemented by a host of other interdenominational agencies of co-operation for such specialized tasks as religious education, home missions, foreign missions, women's work, youth work, etc., and through hundreds of specific union enterprises especially in "mission lands" in such fields as general education, medicine, and theological training, up to the climax of this intricate structure of Christian co-operation in two world Christian bodies rep-

---

[3] If one includes relatively small sects, the total is much larger. On the other hand, it must be noted that some 90 per cent of the Protestant community is found within a dozen or score of major denominational families.

resenting the great bulk of Protestant and several Orthodox communions. Moreover, most of the other world Christian organizations—for students and youth, for Christian education, etc.—plan and work in the closest collaboration with the body that all recognize as the "copestone of the ecumenical arch," the World Council of Churches. Indeed, the formal launching of the World Council at Amsterdam in August, 1948, may be regarded as the placing of that copestone.

In summary: In the first eighteen centuries, frequent and multiplying schisms and scarcely a single concrete achievement of church union; in the last century and a half, some new divisions within Christendom but more than a hundred fully consummated mergers of previously independent national church bodies. Up to the eve of the nineteenth century, scarcely a single organized Christian association across denominational lines; at the middle of the twentieth century, thousands of vigorously functioning agencies of transdenominational collaboration. These are among the facts that justify Sir Ernest Barker's arresting assertion on the eve of the World Christian Conferences at Oxford and Edinburgh in 1937: "Our century has its sad features. But there is one feature in its history which is not sad. That is the gathering tide of Christian union."

II

What has been the role of *Christian missions* in this record of *Christian unity?*

"A Chronology of Christian Unity, 1795–1960," compiled by the William Adams Brown Ecumenical Library in New York, lists 546 events of major importance in the advance of Christian co-operation and church union in the past century and a half. Of these events, 351, or almost two thirds, took place in connection with Christian missions and the younger Christian churches. Furthermore, of the 360 principal incidents of Christian unity involving missions, only 60, or slightly more than a sixth, occurred at what has traditionally been called "the home base," i.e., among the older churches; nearly five sixths occurred on the mission field itself. Here is statistical proof that it has been among the younger churches that the most numerous (and, as we shall presently note, likewise the most difficult and the most important) achievements in Christian unity have been recorded.

A further arresting fact is hidden within these figures. In the early decades, instances of every type of transdenominational co-operation—consultation, comity agreements, co-operative planning, federation, united projects, even church unions—achieved among the older churches of the West outnumbered those on the mission field. In the first fifty years the ratio was ten to four. For example, in the matter of church unions—all within the same communion,[4] to be sure—the first nineteen occurred in Europe and North America. However, by the middle of the nineteenth century, the pendulum had swung decisively. Henceforth, every type of interdenominational collaboration was more numerous, as well as prevailingly more significant, on the mission field. Thus, even a century ago and increasingly since, the fulcrum of Christian unity effort was not merely within the Christian missionary enterprise but also on the scene of the actual operation of missions.

III

When we undertake to survey and summarize this complex of events which constitute the movement for Christian unity, several alternative principles of organization may be proposed.

The story may be told chronologically, tracing the advance of Christian unity year by year and decade after decade through the century and a half.[5] Or the account may follow a geographical pattern, discovering the rise of Christian unity and recounting its progress country by country and area by area across the whole earth.

[4] "Denomination" and "communion" are often confusing terms that are sometimes used interchangeably. "Denomination" properly refers to a particular church body, e.g., the United Lutheran or The Protestant Episcopal Church. "Communion" denotes one of the historic branches of Christendom, e.g., Lutheranism or Anglicanism.

[5] See "A Chronology of Christian Unity, 1795–1960," Appendix I.

There is a third possible method of surveying the data of Christian unity. In some ways, it is more revealing than either the chronological or geographical accounts and it will better serve our purpose.

With all their multiplicity and variety, instances of Christian collaboration fall into six major types, arranged in an ascending order of significance:

   i. *Consultation* for fellowship and mutual counsel.
  ii. *Comity,* i.e., agreement to divide responsibility and eschew overlapping or competition.
 iii. *Co-operation* in joint action.
  iv. *Federation* of churches or church agencies.
   v. *Union institutions.*
  vi. Full organic *church union,* in which the identity of the uniting bodies disappears or is wholly incorporated within the new church.

In terms of this classification, the question can then be asked: Does the total history reveal any drift or trend, any evolution, for example, from the simpler to the more complex expressions of unity, from the more elementary to the more advanced, from the more limited to the more comprehensive, from the easier to the more difficult, from the more trivial to the more significant?

i. Consultation

The earliest instance of interdenominational consultation of which we have record occurred in London in 1819 when the secretaries of the Baptist Missionary Society, the London Missionary Society (itself a nondenominational body),[6] the Church Missionary Society (Anglican), and the Wesleyan Methodist Missionary Society foregathered and agreed to form an "Association" for "mutual counsel and fellowship." The Association continued to meet almost monthly, except during the summers, until World War II. The London Secretaries' Association, however, had no legislative power or authority. Its meetings were quite informal, the mission secretaries coming together regularly simply as individuals for a cup of tea and an informative evening of discussion. Its purpose was limited to fellowship. Yet as years went by, out of these informal contacts there developed a mutual trust and affection so deep that the Association discovered that it could, on occasion, launch projects and initiate undertakings be-

6 See p. 35.

yond its formal authorization. "Gradually, representatives of all missionary societies with headquarters in London joined the pioneering quartet." The three most notable interdenominational missionary conferences in Great Britain in the nineteenth century —Liverpool, 1860; London, 1878; and London, 1888—had their origin in the Secretaries' Association. "And it paved the way for the Conference of Missionary Societies in Great Britain and Ireland, which finally came into being almost a century later, in 1912."[7] Thus, both in its founding and its evolution, the London Secretaries Association was prophetic and representative of a widespread trend.

Almost three quarters of a century was to pass before there was any development in North America parallel to even so modest a venture in missionary consultation as the London Secretaries' Association.[8] Not until 1893 did the corresponding officers of some twenty-three American foreign mission societies gather for a morning and afternoon of conference. On the semicentennial of that occasion, one of the participants, Dr. John R. Mott, recalled the hesitancy, misgiving, and tentativeness with which he and his sixty-seven coconsultants had entered upon so bold an experiment as a day of conversation. So rewarding was the experience that those who attended recommended a similar gathering for the following year. By the fifth of these meetings, the occasion had become known as the Annual Conference of the Foreign Mission Boards but the creation of a Committee of General Reference proved abortive. It was only after fourteen of these yearly consultations, in 1907, that the participants felt emboldened to constitute a Committee on Reference and Counsel as an interim body. Thus, step by step, there came into being in 1911 the Foreign Missions Conference of North America which, in 1950, became the Division of Foreign Missions of the National Council of Churches of Christ in the United States of America. When one contrasts that cautious consultation on January 12, 1893, at the Presbyterian Mission House, 53 Fifth Avenue, New York City, with the unnumbered and globe-encircling enterprises of actual

7 William Richey Hogg, *Ecumenical Foundations* (Harper & Brothers, 1952), pp. 51–53. The pages that follow owe much to Dr. Hogg's chronicle.

8 But a consultation of those concerned for German missions met first in 1846 and was followed in 1885 by the formation of the Committee of the German Evangelical Missions, later the German Missionary Council. See p. 31.

co-operative and united work which are today directed from the Interchurch Center at 475 Riverside Drive, New York City, where several of the denominational missionary agencies as well as the National Council of Churches are headquartered, one sees in epitome something of the advance in Christian unity in Christian missions through the past seven decades.

Tardy as were these American developments, the London initiative of 1819 soon found a response on the mission field. In 1825, missionaries of four societies in Bombay met—the first known occasion of interdenominational Christian consultation on the mission field—and formed the Bombay Missionary Union. Its membership was open to all Protestant missionaries holding "the distinguishing doctrines of the Reformation." Its twofold purpose was to promote Christian fellowship and offer a forum for interchange of experience—a typical illustration of the carefully delimited objectives of those pioneering gatherings.[9]

The Bombay meeting set off something of a chain reaction throughout India. Similar consultations of missionaries of various denominations were held in Madras in 1827 and in Calcutta in 1930. It was a short and logical step to regional meetings although a quarter century elapsed before that step was taken. The earliest of these was the General Conference of Bengal Protestant Missionaries in Calcutta in 1855, to be followed by a parallel conference for missionaries in South India and Ceylon in 1858, and then by the first all-India conference of 1872. Each of these led on to successor gatherings at varied intervals. It was in that latter year, 1872, that the first important consultation of missionaries outside India occurred, in Japan. Similar gatherings in other widely scattered lands followed—in the Netherlands Indies in 1881 (but following an initial meeting in 1855), and in Mexico in 1888. After the turn of the century, conferences of missionaries in various areas multiplied, especially in Africa south of the Sahara. Most of these assembled periodically. Most of them have followed the precedent of the London Secretaries' Association in discovering that they could "on occasion launch projects and initiate undertakings beyond what they were technically capable of doing." Indeed, most of them have developed over the years from mere consultations, in the direction of federations. Many ultimately became the national Christian councils in over fifty countries today.

[9] Hogg, *op. cit.*, p. 18.

It is noteworthy that the earliest interdenominational consultations on the mission field, indeed the first eight, should have taken place in India. This was prophetic of the leadership of Christians in India in every phase and type of *Christian unity* that has continued to this day. How is this priority of India to be explained? In part by the fact that Christian missions were of earlier origin in India than elsewhere. Partly also because of the urgent need for consultation in the face of pressing difficulties for missionary advance in the trying circumstances of Indian life. But it was also an evidence of the special conviction regarding *Christian unity* that has characterized both missionaries and nationals in India from earliest days. This in turn was doubtless in some measure a reaction to the pluralistic religious situation in India and the widely prevalent tendencies toward syncretism. Pagan syncretism could be effectively countered only by a single interpretation of Christian faith no less than by a united deployment of Christian resources. Probably not less influential was the vision and voice of a single man, at once a pioneer missionary in India and, no less, the pioneer prophet of missionary co-operation and union. As early as 1806, William Carey, "the father of modern missions," had urged the calling of a world conference, "a general association of all denominations of Christians from the four quarters of the world to meet at the Cape of Good Hope in 1810 and decennially thereafter." Carey's suggestion was both so revolutionary and so farsighted that it merits reproduction in full. It was embodied in a letter to Andrew Fuller, Secretary of the Baptist Missionary Society in London, written from Calcutta on May 15, 1806:

> The Cape of Good Hope is now in the hands of the English; should it continue so, would it not be possible to have a general association of all denominations of Christians, from the four quarters of the world, kept there once in about ten years? I earnestly recommend this plan, let the first meeting be in the year 1810, or 1812 at furthest. I have no doubt but it would be attended with very important effects; we could understand one another better, and more entirely enter into one another's views by two hours conversation than by two or three years epistolary correspondence.[10]

Andrew Fuller characterized this suggestion as "one of brother

10 Compare *A History of the Ecumenical Movement, 1517–1948,* edited by Ruth Rouse and Stephen Charles Neill (The Westminster Press, 1954), p. 355, n. 2.

Carey's pleasing dreams."[11] Carey's proposal was dismissed as visionary, impractical, and fruitless. It was to see fulfillment in almost exactly the terms that Carey had envisioned just a century later, at Edinburgh in 1910, and in the sequence of world missionary conferences that have followed roughly decennially since —Jerusalem, 1928; Madras, 1938; Whitby, 1947; Willingen, 1952; Ghana, 1958.

Those early Indian consultations were marked by a novel and extraordinary spirit. Of one of them William Carey wrote: "No shadow of bigotry falls on us here. It would have done your heart good to have joined us. . . . In these meetings the utmost harmony prevails and a union of hearts unknown between persons of different denominations in England."[12] Moreover, they were studded by incidents of the keenest interest. For example, at the Bengal Conference at Lahore in 1862, a corporate Communion service was held, administered by a Presbyterian clergyman through Baptist deacons in which Anglicans and Methodists as well as Presbyterians and Baptists partook. At the same meeting, a proposal for an Indian Catholic Church provoked the largest response and hope. The South India Conference at Bangalore in 1879 likewise anticipated a "church of Christ in India," not to see fulfillment until sixty-eight years later.

Moreover, through the sequence of pioneering meetings in India, progress in the techniques of effective conference organization and administration is clearly discernible. Gatherings of individuals open to any who cared to attend were succeeded by formal conventions of officially appointed delegates. Assemblies to listen to addresses and papers gave place to work sessions in committees, preceded by careful preparation. Thus, steps of advance to be traversed much later at the home base were being prospected, and tried and tested methods were being established for subsequent world-wide employment. In all of them, "comity and co-operation" unfailingly appeared on the agenda, usually as the last and climactic topic.

Whatever the explanation, history records that India has been and continues in the forefront of the quest for Christian unity. It is no accident that the earliest instance of interdenominational church union in history should have been achieved in India—

[11] Norman Goodall, *The Ecumenical Movement* (Oxford University Press, 1961), p. 5.
[12] *Ibid.*

the union of Presbyterians and Congregationalists in 1908 to form the United Church of South India, itself prophetic of the larger and far more significant union, of which it was one of the constituents, into the Church of South India in 1947.

It is no accident that the most passionate and moving plea for church union ever formulated by official church representatives—that of the younger churchmen at Tambaram in 1938—should have been issued in India through the voice of an Indian Christian who himself had proved an unwavering advocate of the cause since Edinburgh, 1910, the late Bishop Azariah:

> The representatives of the younger churches in this section, one and all gave expression to the passionate longing that exists in all countries for visible union of the churches. . . . Visible and organic union must be our goal. . . . Such a union alone will remove the evils arising out of our divisions. . . . Loyalty, however, will forbid the younger churches' going forward to consummate any union unless it receives the wholehearted support and blessing of those through whom these churches have been planted. We are thus often torn between loyalty to our mother churches and loyalty to our ideal of union. We, therefore, appeal with all the fervor we possess, to the missionary societies and boards and the responsible authorities of the older churches, to take this matter seriously to heart, to labor with the churches in the mission field to achieve this union, to support and encourage us in all our efforts to put an end to the scandalous effects of our divisions and to lead us in the path of union—the union for which our Lord prayed, through which the world would indeed believe in the Divine Mission of the Son, our Lord Jesus Christ.[13]

It is no accident that the most notable single achievement of church union is that of the Church of South India, in no small measure the handiwork of Bishop Azariah, and that the two most important pending proposals for church union should be in North India and Ceylon. These are late expressions of a concern that, for more than a century, has never lain dormant in that land. Certainly when the definitive chronicle of Christian unity is written, it will be recorded that Indian Christianity is to be recognized as the mother of Christian unity, and it may well be that India's greatest contribution will have been in this area.

In Japan, China, Latin America, Africa, and the Near East,

---

[13] *The World Mission of the Church* (International Missionary Council, 1939), p. 130. Compare the statement by younger church representatives at the successor International Missionary Council meeting at Willengen in 1952. *The Missionary Obligation of the Church.* Edinburgh House Press, 1952.

history has repeated nearly identical patterns. The first consultation in Japan, a local gathering of missionaries in Yokohama in 1872,[14] resolved unanimously to work for a catholic "Church of Christ" in Japan. It was followed by a General Conference of Protestant Missionaries in 1883. This in turn was the precursor of what became annual meetings. Similarly, in China, a consultation in Shanghai in 1877 led to a series of General Conferences with Christian unity as a major theme, and the formation of a Christian Federation of China as an eventual, inevitable proposal. The story in Latin America, starting with an assembly in Mexico City in 1888, in various parts of Africa beginning with the Nyasaland United Missionary Conference of 1900, and in lands of the Moslem world from the Cairo Conference of 1906 onward, is much the same. At the second general conference of missionaries in British East Africa (Kenya) at Kikuyu in 1913, two bishops of the Church of England shared in a service of inter-Communion conducted according to the Anglican *Book of Common Prayer* but held in a mission of the Church of Scotland with non-Anglicans participating. The protest of the Anglo-Catholic Bishop of Zanzibar was carried to the Lambeth Conference; although the latter declined to sustain charges of heresy and schism, Anglican participation in inter-Communion was halted. Here, once more, we meet an incident that was all too prophetic: a bold initiative on the mission field is discouraged and negated by the traditionalism and conservatism of the parent church of the West.

In the meantime, developments at the home base for the most part followed those in the more progressive mission fields. In 1837, secretaries of four German societies and the Paris mission met at Basel. In 1846, the first important interdenominational conference in support of German missions assembled in Berlin, to be followed four decades later, in 1885, by the formation of the Committee of the German Evangelical Missions, which became the German Missionary Council. Representatives of the several Scandinavian missionary bodies came together for consultation periodically through the 1850's and 1860's. These were followed by the earliest similar gatherings in Anglo-Saxon lands, in New

---

[14] "The senior members of the Presbyterian, Reformed, and Congregational missions formed the voting nucleus. The chief purpose was to standardize the scattered efforts at New Testament translation." Charles W. Iglehart, *A Century of Protestant Christianity in Japan* (Charles E. Tuttle Company, 1959), pp. 42 f.

York and London in 1854, the precursors of the series meeting roughly decennially that culminated in Edinburgh, 1910. However, these were large assemblies for public addresses rather than consultation. As we have already noted, it was not until 1893 that the North American Continent witnessed a consultation comparable to those which had been meeting regularly in India for nearly half a century and in Japan and China for two decades. Moreover, in imagination of conception, frankness in discussion, soundness in organization and procedure, boldness of vision, and fruitfulness in action, the many widely scattered consultations throughout Asia during the preceding fifty years stand in sharp contrast to the cautious timidity that characterized that first and historic American meeting.

ii. Comity

At the Edinburgh Conference of 1910, Commission VIII on "Co-operation and the Promotion of Unity" began the introduction to its report with this observation:

> Before either co-operation or unity can be looked for, that spirit of considerateness, fair-dealing, Christian courtesy, and brotherliness, which is called "Comity," must be prevalent. . . . We shall deal under the general title of "Comity" with agreements reached between different societies as to the delimitation of territory and other matters on which a common understanding is reached apart from direct co-operation in practical work.[15]

Just twenty-five years later, the editors of the *Conspectus of Co-operative Missionary Enterprises* (1935) could remark: "Comity and the principle of division of territory are taken for granted now by most boards and their missions."[16]

As a matter of fact, the Edinburgh Commission somewhat underestimated the extent and significance of the collaboration already achieved; in some instances it had gone beyond mere consultation or even comity to elementary forms of co-operation. Nevertheless, broadly speaking, the principal objective of missionary consultations throughout the nineteenth century, so far as the mission boards were concerned, was the achievement of comity—a high-sounding aphorism for avoidance of competition,

15 Quoted by Charles H. Fahs and Helen E. Davis in *Conspectus of Co-operative Missionary Enterprises* (International Missionary Council, 1935), p. 1.
16 *Ibid.*, p. 2.

as Commission VIII at Edinburgh suggested, "co-operation on its more negative side."[17]

Probably the earliest statement of the obligation to comity was the resolution of the American Board of Commissioners for Foreign Missions in 1838: "Resolved: That . . . wherever a society has a mission already in a district or country where another society contemplates operations, it be deemed suitable that the societies whose missionaries are already in the field be apprised of the fact and consulted before such operations are commenced." Here, comity might perhaps more precisely be denominated "courtesy"—a very modest dimension of Christian courtesy, indeed.

However, as Dr. H. Paul Douglass has pointed out, the latter half of the nineteenth century was not predominantly a period of advance in Christian co-operation or comity, or even courtesy. In the United States it was marked by theological controversy and denominational schism due in part, of course, to political factors, especially the American Civil War. In Great Britain, likewise, the latter decades of the century were a period of regression rather than advance in Christian co-operation and effort for Christian unity.[18] The Centenary Conference of Protestant Missions in London, in 1888, could venture no more than this qualified assertion of progress in comity during the preceding century, which it was commemorating: "Concord is greater than discord; and respect for one another's boundaries more general than refraction of them."[19] This statement furnishes a chastening disclosure as to the limited extent of missionary co-operation near the close of the nineteenth century.

Nevertheless, comity had been a continuing preoccupation of the ever-multiplying missionary conferences, at home and abroad. The initial Union Missionary Convention of 1854 in New York gave its attention to this as one of eight questions on its agenda:

> IV. In view of the great extent of the heathen world, and the degrees to which it is opened, is it expedient for different missionary boards to plant stations on the same ground?

[17] *Co-operation and Unity,* Report of Commission VIII, Edinburgh, 1910, p. 13.

[18] Compare Norman Goodall's forthcoming volume, *The Ecumenical Movement,* pp. 101 ff.

[19] Quoted by H. Paul Douglass in "Christian Unity and the Younger Churches," *Christendom* (Summer, 1940), p. 415.

On the mission field, however, comity was less a topic for discussion than an imperative for agreement and implementation. Moreover, there was no doubt as to where the problem of overlapping and even occasional conflict and competition was felt to center and where, if at all, it must receive solution. These unseemly and unworthy features of the missionary work of different churches and societies were direct projections of inexcusable deficiency in consultation and agreement at the home base. The 1858 South India and Ceylon Conference of Missionaries dispatched a vigorous protest to the Leipzig Mission for its failure to observe general rules of comity practiced by other societies. The earliest missionary conferences in Mexico in the 1880's and 1890's were primarily occupied with "pressing matters of comity." As we have observed, "comity and co-operation" well-nigh invariably appeared as one item on the agendas of missionary conferences throughout Asia, not infrequently as the last item, a position that the various issues of Christian unity have traditionally occupied. Hogg rightly summarizes the matter thus:

> Comity, except for the Moslem workers' conference (where it had been affirmed that "comity . . . was no problem"), frequently divided territory among societies. Comity also included inter-mission agreements on the salaries of employed nationals and the qualifications for church membership and transfer.

But the missionaries themselves were not satisfied with formal agreements. Agencies of mediation, if not of enforcement, were required and created:

> One also observes the frequent demand for a continuing board of arbitration or appeal to deal with the situation in which two or more missions might find themselves at loggerheads.

And in India, Japan, China, South Africa, and Mexico, such boards of appeal were established.[20]

Apparently the arranging of comity was a major objective in the formation of the early national Christian councils. The advance, both in the functions of these councils and in the work that they sought to promote, is disclosed in this terse statement: "These earlier encouraged comity and latterly have served as the national interdenominational organs of the younger churches."[21]

20 Hogg, *op. cit.*, pp. 33–34.
21 *Ibid.*, p. 571.

Consultation in furtherance of comity led on to the next stage—co-operation, that is, joint action.

iii. Co-operation

Here we are confronted by a seeming paradox. If logic alone determined historic events, we should expect to find ourselves passing in neat chronological sequence from *consultation* through *comity* to *co-operation*, and we should discover the latter transition occurring close to the last turn of the century. As we shall see, in broad perspective this expectation is not altogether mistaken.

However, when we seek for the first concrete instance of significant transdenominational Christian co-operation, we find it, not at the dawn of the twentieth century but at the close of the eighteenth, not as a sequel to consultation and comity but as their precursor. The date most often named for the beginning of the modern Christian unity movement is 1795. In that year communicants of the Church of England, of the established Church of Scotland, and of English Independent and Methodist bodies—acting, to be sure, not as representatives of their respective churches but as individual Christians joined forces to form the London Missionary Society. How unprecedented and momentous was this event is suggested in the impression made upon one of the participants:

> We have now before us a blessed spectacle—Christians of different denominations, although differing in points of church government, united in forming a society for propagating the gospel among the heathen. This is a new thing in the Christian church. . . . Here are Episcopalians, Methodists, Presbyterians, and Independents, all united in one society, all joining to form its laws, to regulate its institutions and manage its various concerns. Behold us here assembled with one accord to attend the funeral of bigotry.[22]

It is noteworthy that that event was not at the simplest, easiest, most elementary and trivial level, that of *consultation*, but at the much higher and more difficult level of *co-operation;* and that it occurred not on the mission field but at the home base, although it was motivated solely by concern for the more effective prosecution of overseas missions. This observation places a salutary check on any too simple and neat portrayal of the total development in

[22] Quoted by Gaius Jackson Slosser, *Christian Unity* (E. P. Dutton & Co., Inc., 1929), p. 119.

terms of advance from lower to higher stages. Three facts about
the London Missionary Society deserve note: (1) Initially it was
wholly unofficial in sponsorship. (2) Although thoroughly nondenominational in origin, it eventually became an agency primarily of one of the participating groups, the English Congregationalists. (3) Most important, the motive for collaboration was
a more effective discharge of missionary responsibility.

The inauguration of the London Missionary Society in 1795
in no sense stood alone. In the following year, Presbyterians,
Baptists, and Reformed joined to form the New York Missionary
Society for work among American Indians. The year 1804 marked
the launching of the Religious Tract Society, and of the British
and Foreign Bible Society. Six years later on the North American
Continent came the projection of the American Board of Commissioners for Foreign Missions—on the initiative of Congregationalist, Presbyterian, and Reformed churchmen; and after
another six years, the American Bible Society. Both of these
American organizations were closely akin to their British counter-
parts. How epochal were these organizations in the thought of
those who founded them is indicated in this description of the
meeting that initiated the British and Foreign Bible Society:
"Surrounded by a multitude of Christians, whose doctrines and
ritualistic differences had for ages kept them asunder, and who
had been taught to regard each other with a sort of pious es-
trangement, or rather of concentrated hostility, the scene was
new."[23] In 1815, the Basel Evangelical Missionary Society with
Lutheran and Reformed members was founded; in 1822, the
Paris Evangelical Missionary Society, and in 1828, the Rhenish
Missionary Association, also embracing Lutherans and Reformed.

However, these notable events serve less to invalidate our
logical order than to underscore one of the most important facts
in the entire history of both missions and Christian unity, and
especially their interrelations. None of the nine bodies just named
was, properly speaking, interdenominational, for none was the
creation of a denomination or group of denominations. Each was
brought into being by *individual Christians,* though of different
denominational affiliations, who acted not in behalf of, but in
independence of, their respective churches. They were *nondenominational* not interdenominational. Moreover, the London
Missionary Society and the American Board, although initiated

23 *History of the British and Foreign Bible Society,* I, 44.

by Christians of several churches, eventually virtually became agencies of a single denomination as denominational missionary societies gradually came into existence, largely stimulated by the example of the earlier nondenominational bodies, and drew away the support of all except the Congregationalists. The most significant point, however, is that while the churches were still at the stage of consultation concerned mainly with comity—indeed, decades before the churches had achieved that most elementary level of Christian collaboration—their more prophetic and resolute members were busily engaged in actual co-operation in united work.

Nevertheless, that is not the whole story of co-operation in the nineteenth century. During that same century, so largely characterized by elementary efforts at the home base, co-operation in joint enterprises had gone long distances on the mission field itself. As early as 1844, the East China Religious Tract Society, precursor of the Chinese Religious Tract Society, was founded. Even more epochal was the launching of the Zenana Bible and Medical Mission,[24] founded in 1852 by Anglicans, Baptists, Congregationalists, Methodists, and Presbyterians. It is worthy of special comment that this occurred on the initiative of women, that its field of service was India, and that its primary purpose was educational, more specifically the education of women. The year 1858 saw the initiation of the Christian Vernacular Education Society (forerunner of the Christian Literature Society) also in India. And in 1863, Robert College was founded at Constantinople (Istanbul) as a nondenominational Christian institution for higher education. The year 1876 saw two further pioneering events in India. The India Sunday School Union was inaugurated and the Madras Christian College became a union institution. Each of the six organizations just named was prophetic of contrasted types of Christian co-operation on the mission field that were to multiply in succeeding decades across the world—the nondenominational *tract society,* the *medical mission,* the *literature society,* the *Christian college,* the *Sunday school union,* and the *interdenominationally sponsored school or college.*

To recount, instance by instance, the step-by-step advance in Christian co-operation in well-nigh every missionary area would exhaust patience as well as exceed the limits of space. It must suffice to call attention to three additional types of *inter*denomi-

[24] Now called the Bible and Medical Missionary Fellowship.

national co-operation that arose after the turn of the century, each more difficult and more significant than any thus far listed, and to name their earliest examples—interdenominational *theological education* of which the Union Theological Seminaries of Manila and Indore, Central India (both 1907), appear to be the forerunners; the *national Christian council,* anticipated in the Evangelical Union of the Philippines in 1901, the Federation of Evangelical Churches of Puerto Rico in 1905, and the Federal Council of Churches in Korea in 1918; and, finally and climactically, the *United Church* again pioneered in India in the union of 1908 of Congregationalists, Presbyterians, and Reformed to create the South India United Church. The latter anticipated by some thirteen years the earliest church union across denominational lines in the West.[25]

It is some measure of the spread of all these forms of co-operation that, by 1934, their institutions numbered over four hundred. By then, many that had initially been *non*denominational had become *inter*denominational. Many later ones were interdenominational from the outset. Indeed, not a few of them express such a complete merging of the resources as well as the interests of the cosponsoring churches that they are, in effect, organic unions—not, to be sure of whole church bodies—but of these church bodies in their actual functioning in specific projects. As such, we shall revert to them in our discussion of union institutions.

iv. Federation

When we pass on to the next higher level of *Christian unity,* that of federation, i.e., the association of churches or church agencies for multiple and diverse united undertakings, the later realizations of full-blown church federation, had very early anticipations on the mission field, e.g., the Evangelical Union of the Philippines (1901), the Federation of Christian Missions in Japan (1902), the National Missionary Society of India (1905), the Federation of Evangelical Churches of Puerto Rico (1905), and the General Council of Evangelical Missions in Korea (1905). These bodies may rightly be viewed as precursors of the more developed and significant church federations of recent decades.

I have not been able to discover whether these early missionary

25 The United Church of Canada, 1925.

pathfinders had a direct influence, at least by way of suggestion and example, upon the authors and architects of the Federal Council of Churches of Christ in America. In any event, the latter body, founded in 1908, deserves a place of special recognition in the chronicles of Christian unity. To be sure, it had been pre-ceded by the National Federation of Churches and Christian Workers in 1900, but this was an association of individuals and a few farsighted congregations.[26] The Federal Council was the first formal association of denominational church bodies any-where in the world for the prosecution of common tasks. The Federal Council falls outside the limits of our inquiry. But be-cause of its immense influence, not only as the pioneer of Chris-tian councils elsewhere among both older and younger churches but also as pattern for the several ecumenical bodies that led up to the World Council of Churches, it merits special mention.

The example of the American Federal Council has worked out across the face of the earth to inspire the formation of similar federations or councils of churches in sixty-eight lands, three fourths of them among the younger churches. It has also worked downward in the United States to prompt the proliferation of state, county, and local councils of churches to the present as-tounding total of almost one thousand.

The parallel development on the mission field dates, for all practical purposes, from the great and fecund World Missionary Conference at Edinburgh in 1910. The Continuation Committee authorized at Edinburgh met at Lake Mohonk in the United States in 1912. Immediately thereafter, Dr. John R. Mott set forth on a long trip through Asia. He convened no fewer than twenty-one regional conferences from Colombo to Tokyo, attended by nearly sixteen hundred participants of whom 35 per cent were Asians and 14 per cent women. A number of these conferences followed the example of Edinburgh by setting up continuation committees or national missionary councils. But these were still preponderantly councils of *missions* along the lines of those which had earlier been formed in the Philippines, Japan, India, Puerto Rico, and Korea, although Japan had already in 1911 taken a farther step forward by creating the Federation of Churches in Japan.[27]

[26] John A. Hutchison, *We Are Not Divided* (Round Table Press, Inc., 1941), pp. 26, 32.

[27] Hogg, *op. cit.*, pp. 151–156.

The organization of the International Missionary Council (it-self the earliest achievement of world federation) in 1921 led to other embassies to the Orient by Dr. Mott in that and the following years. As far back as 1909 when he was deeply in-volved in preparing the Edinburgh Conference the following year, Dr. Mott had been invited to become the first Executive Secretary of the American Federal Council.[28] Almost certainly, therefore, Dr. Mott carried the example of the Federal Council in his mind, possibly the pattern of the Federal Council in his brief case, as he set off for Asia. His journey—one of the most important among the many in his long career as unofficial Am-bassador Plenipotentiary of Christian Unity—had, as its most significant fruitage, the organization of the National Christian Council of India, Burma, and Ceylon (1922), the National Christian Council of China (1922), and the National Christian Council of Japan (1923), all of them developments of the Con-tinuation Committees created ten years earlier.

The following two decades, up to the outbreak of World War II, witnessed the creation of councils, some of them still missions councils but many national Christian councils in thirteen younger-church lands: Sierra Leone, 1924; Korea, 1924; the Congo, 1924; the Near East, 1927; Mexico, 1927; the Philip-pines, 1929; the Gold Coast (now Ghana), 1929; Siam (now Thailand), 1929; Nigeria, 1930; Brazil, 1934; South Africa, 1936; Trinidad and Tobago, 1936; Argentina (the River Plate), 1939. These, together with the National Christian Councils of India, China, and Japan, and the Association of Evangelical Churches of Puerto Rico, which dated from 1905, brought the total of councils in Asia, Africa, and Latin America on the eve of World War II to seventeen. But in countries of the older churches in Europe and North America, only six analogous councils were to be discovered—in the United States (1908), in England (1919), in Finland (1920), in Switzerland (1920), in Belgium (1923), and in the Netherlands (1935).

The proposal to create a world council of churches (in 1937) prompted a quick and vigorous response in all parts of the world. Although World War II intervened almost immediately, it seemed to encourage rather than retard the formation of Chris-tian councils on every continent. Indeed, there is no more strik-

28 Basil Mathews, *John R. Mott, World Citizen* (Harper & Brothers, 1934), p. 435.

ing and heartening testimony to the resolve and strength of the ecumenical impulse than the fact that the very years when the nations were embroiled in the fiercest internecine struggle of history recorded the launching of no fewer than sixteen new national organs of Christian co-operation, twelve in younger-church areas: Jamaica, 1939; Peru, 1940; Chile, 1941; Algeria, 1941; Cuba, 1941; Nyasaland, 1942; Surinam, 1943; Kenya, 1943; Mozambique, 1944; Northern Rhodesia, 1944; Honduras, 1945; Ceylon, 1945; and four in countries directly involved in the conflict: New Zealand (1941), Great Britain (1942), Hungary (1944), and Canada (1944). This brought the total of councils among the younger churches to twenty-nine and among the older churches to ten—thirty-nine in all.

In the fifteen years since the war's terminus, the proliferation of national councils has continued apace. In Africa, Asia, and Latin America, twenty-two have been inaugurated or transformed from missions councils: West Africa, 1945; Northern Sudan, 1947; Malaya, 1948; Tanganyika, 1948; Burma, 1949; Ecuador, 1949; Pakistan, 1949; Colombia, 1950; Indonesia, 1950; Costa Rica, 1950; Iran, 1951; Guatemala, 1953; Southwest Asia, 1953; Hong-kong, 1954; Angola, 1954; Southern Rhodesia, 1954; Bolivia, 1955; Uruguay, 1956; Cameroons and Equatorial Africa, 1957; Okinawa, 1958; Israel, 1958; Madagascar, 1958. To round out the picture, mention should be made of a number of looser bodies, usually federations of missions rather than full-fledged national Christian councils, some of them occupying a position midway between missionary conferences and Christian councils, for example, in Ethiopia and Egypt; a few of those listed above are in transition from the earlier to the more mature status.

In the meantime, the roll of councils in Europe, Australasia, and North America has been increased by additions in Poland (1945), Italy (1946), Australia (1946), Germany (1948), Czechoslovakia (1956), Austria (1958), and Denmark (1959).

The upshot of this movement of federation in lands of the younger churches through the past half century is today an aggregate of fifty-one Christian councils in Africa, Asia, and Latin America. This figure contrasts strikingly with a total of seventeen similar bodies among the older churches of Europe, North America, and Australasia. At every point in this phase of Christian unity, Christain missions and the churches to which they gave birth have led the way for the ancient churches of the West.

v. Union Institutions

Intermediate between co-operation and church union stands
still another expression of *Christian unity* of such extent and
practical significance and influence as to warrant a separate classification—union institutions. Formally, the participating churches
or church agencies co-operate to sponsor and sustain a particular
piece of work unitedly. But, in their most highly developed and
representative illustrations, these enterprises represent the full
and complete union of the participating bodies *for the purposes
in view*. That is to say, the supporting bodies delegate determination of policies, appointments, budgets, etc., i.e., sovereignty, to
an interdenominational organization on which each is represented
but which none by itself can control. It cannot be questioned that
these union enterprises, now to be numbered by the scores if not
hundreds, many of them so functioning as unions for many decades, must be recognized as among the strongest, most effective,
and most influential arms of the Christian church at work in the
world. No less important, in not a few cases they have served as
anticipations of the full organic union of their sponsoring churches
and as training grounds for leadership of united churches.

The pioneers in this type of united action were mentioned at
the end of our survey of co-operation. An early illustration is the
Religious Tract Society, anticipated in East China in 1844. Another instance, also concerned with the more adequate provision
of materials for Christian nurture and education, is the *Christian
Literature Society,* anticipated by the Christian Vernacular Education Society of India in 1858. Both of these types were doubtless
inspired by the nondenominational Bible societies, which had
been operating at the home base since the earliest years of the
nineteenth century and which themselves have become increasingly agencies of the churches. The epochal significance of the
Zenana Bible and Medical Mission, founded by Anglicans, Baptists, Congregationalists, Methodists, and Presbyterians in 1852,
has also been noted. One of the most significant events in this
area was the transformation of the Madras Christian College into
a *union institution* in 1876, establishing a precedent for *union
educational institutions* at all levels and in almost every major
area of the world. Once again, India was in the lead.

However, if one were asked to identify the particular type of
union institution that has exerted the largest influence upon
the over-all advance of Christian unity, there could hardly be

question. The *interdenominational theological school,* beginning
with Manila and Indore in Central India in 1907, now numbers
the overwhelming majority of the strongest training schools for
the ministry among the younger churches—Union Seminary,
Manila, and Silliman in the Philippine Islands; Union Seminary,
Tokyo and Doshisha in Japan; Nanking Theological Seminary
and others in China; Trinity College, Singapore; United Theological College, Bangalore, and a half dozen others of the leading
seminaries in India; Near East School of Theology, Beirut; Evangelical Theological Seminary of Puerto Rico; Union Evangelical
Seminary, Mexico; Union Theological Seminary, Buenos Aires,
to mention only a few of the best known. Here, the future leadership of churches of different denominational affiliations receive
almost identical preparation for their several ministries and live
and worship within a living ecumenical Christian community.
Inevitably, a large proportion of those who direct the various
types of co-operative, federated, and union efforts are products of
such transdenominational training. More than that, it is not to
be wondered that many of those so trained, having experienced
the reality of Christian unity during these formative years of
preparation, become convinced, ardent, and lifelong workers for
the unity of Christ's church.

By 1934, union institutions of the several types in younger-
church areas had multiplied to the number of 121. (In every instance, collaboration of churches of the same denominational
family is disregarded. Only union institutions involving the full
merging of resources by churches of different denominational
families are in view.) These 121 projects may be classified as
follows: higher education, 20; medical schools, 4; other medical
institutions (hospitals, etc.), 12; theological schools and seminaries, 19; teacher training institutions, 4; Bible schools, 9;
junior colleges and middle schools, 16; normal schools, 9; schools
for missionary children, 4; union churches, 6; miscellaneous, 18.

No comparable figures for 1960 have been compiled. But the
total must be very much larger by now. For example, in 1955,
nondenominational and interdenominational institutions of
higher education totaled ninety.

As a single illustration, one may cite the United Board for
Christian Colleges in China.[29] Until the communist take-over,

[29] Now the United Board for Christian Higher Education in Asia, sponsored by twenty-one boards representing fifteen churches and three colleges
from the United States, Canada, and Great Britain.

the United Board represented the merging of direction, support, and personnel by more than a dozen church mission boards and a number of independent missionary agencies in North America for the single purpose of furthering Christian higher education in China, conducted in nine union colleges and universities in that land.

vi. Church Union

In the climactic expression of Christian unity—organic church union—the general pattern has been repeated. The earliest church unions, the first nineteen, all occurred between older churches. But every one of these involved merely the reunion within the same family of branches that had separated over an intrafamily quarrel.

As we have seen the earliest union to bring together churches from contrasted family traditions was on the mission field, once again in India—the *South India United Church,* formed in 1908 by the merger of Congregational, Presbyterian, and Reformed bodies, and itself one of the three constituents of the larger and vastly more significant *Church of South India* in 1947. In 1924, the same denominations—Congregational and Presbyterian—united to form the *United Church of Northern India,* further enlarged in 1938 and 1945. In 1927 came the *Church of Christ in China,* embracing, in addition to Presbyterians and Congregationalists, some Baptists, some Methodists, Evangelical United Brethren, and later Evangelical and Reformed and the United Church of Canada. Two years later, in 1929, Congregationalists and Presbyterians again joined with United Brethren to create the *United Evangelical Church of the Philippines* to be later enlarged by the inclusion of Disciples of Christ and some Methodists. In 1931, United Brethren and Christians and Congregationalists formed the *United Evangelical Church in Puerto Rico.* In 1934, Baptists in Siam united with Presbyterians in the *Church of Christ in Siam* (Thailand). In 1936, the *Evangelical Church in Guatemala* joined Presbyterians with the Central American Mission. In 1941 came the *Church of Christ in Japan,* reconstituted after the conclusion of World War II into the present Kyodan; its present membership includes all or part of some fifteen previously independent churches and embraces just about one half of all Protestants in Japan. In 1945, Congregationalists and Presbyterians once more joined forces in the Copper Belt to constitute the *Church of Central Africa* in Rhodesia.

In summary, of the eighteen unions across denominational barriers in Christian history, thirteen have been achieved among younger Christian churches. Among these are embraced two of the three that by general acknowledgment are the most significant—the Church of South India and the Church of Christ in Japan.[30] Among further unions at present under promising negotiation, by all odds the two of largest import likewise involve younger churches—that in Northern India and that in Ceylon.

IV

This concludes our survey of *Christian unity* in *Christian missions* over the past century and a half.

Our purpose has been to gain some impression of the over-all sweep of a historic trend. We began with the query whether such an inquiry might disclose any drift or evolution within the development. In that perspective, three conclusions stand forth upon the record:

1. There has been evolution, from the simpler to the more complex expressions of unity, from the more elementary to the more advanced, from the more limited to the more comprehensive, from the easier to the more difficult, from the more trivial to the more significant. *Consultation* for the sake of *comity* has gone forward to elementary *co-operation* in common tasks. This has led to the creation of continuing and comprehensive organs of joint action, both *federations* or *councils* and *union institutions*. The latter have prepared the way for full and permanent *church unions*. These, in turn, began as *re*unions of separate branches of the same denominational family, but have latterly been overshadowed in both numbers and importance by mergers between churches representative of diverse historic traditions and affinities. Here is impressive evidence of progress, of the working of the Spirit of God in the total development.

---

[30] The third is the United Church of Canada formed in 1925 by a union of Congregationalists, Methodists, and Presbyterians. Next in inclusiveness and significance would appear to be the United Church of Christ in the United States.

2. In virtually every phase of *Christian unity,* the pioneering initiative was taken *not* by church bodies or their official representatives but by Christian individuals, not infrequently laymen, who although devout and loyal churchmen, acted outside of and often in spite of institutional church structures or even the approval of their spokesmen.

3. With respect to every major type of collaboration, the originating impulses sprang out of the life, needs, and convictions of the Christian world mission. And the earliest fulfillments establishing precedents for both younger and older churches were achievements of the Christian world mission.

These are the facts that support our earlier generalization: in almost every particular, the Christian world mission has been both precursor and progenitor of the movement for Christian unity.

PART II

Today:

The Younger Churches and Christian Unity

I

In Part I, we were concerned solely with historical background. Our purpose was to be able to see the world Christian movement today in perspective. To that end, we attempted to survey the most significant developments in Christianity in the last one hundred and fifty years.

From even so cursory a survey, certain facts stand forth, three in particular:

1. Over the past century and a half, Christianity has swept in ever wider circles across the face of the earth. No other movement in history has ever advanced so fast or so far. It has claimed to its adherence ever larger numbers and an ever larger proportion of mankind—today, about eight hundred and fifty million or roughly one third of the human race. No other movement in history has ever won the allegiance of so many or so large a proportion of humanity. Moreover, the evidence is strong that, during this same period, Christianity has exerted, directly and indirectly, a deeper and more pervasive influence for good upon the life of all sorts and conditions of men than it had exerted in any previous epoch of Christian history or, indeed, than had ever been wrought by any other corporate force in any comparable period. In summary, this has been "the epoch of largest, most varied, and most notable achievement" by the Christian religion in its two thousand years of history. These are the facts that justify our foremost Christian historian's designation of this as "The Great Century" (1815–1914).

2. Christian advance during that period has moved forward along two sharply contrasted, largely independent, and yet complementary lines:

a. The modern *movement of Christian missions* which has carried the Christian message to the outermost parts of the earth with the result that Christianity has become for the first time and at long last a world faith—the only candidate save communism for recognition as a universal faith.

b. The effort for *Christian unity,* moving forward by many paths, but two in particular and of largest importance:

49

(1) *Church union,* i.e., the actual permanent merger of previously separate and independent national church bodies. One hundred such organic church unions have been achieved in the past century and a half in contrast to one church union in the previous eighteen centuries. Moreover, as we noted, there has been a logic of advance within these one hundred unions, from the simpler to the more complex, from the easier to the more difficult, from the less to the more significant, from reunions of branches of the same denominational family to comprehensive mergers of churches from two or more contrasted historic types.

(2) *Interchurch association and co-operation,* in an intricate network of organs of collaboration, especially councils of churches by which most of the major branches of Christianity—except the Church of Rome, two large American Protestant denominations (Southern Baptists and Missouri Synod Lutherans), and a number of relatively new and rapidly multiplying Evangelical Christian groups—are today linked in intimate association for united action at every level, in local communities, in states and nations, on a world scale.

We have suggested that it is these two developments together which give to this period of a century and a half a character as distinctive and a significance as distinguished as any previous so-called "Great Age" of Christian faith. It is these two together which today constitute what is known as "ecumenical Christianity."

These two major developments—*Christian missions* and *Christian unity,* although in many respects sharply contrasted, have themselves been drawing steadily and at a steadily accelerating pace closer together. Each of them finds expression in a world Christian body—the International Missionary Council and the World Council of Churches—which today function as two complementary arms of a single organism, ecumenical Christianity, world-wide and united. At this moment, they are planning still closer organic association through the "integration" of these two world organizations into a more comprehensive World Council of Churches.

3. Within these facts, indeed in some ways their most unexpected and also their most significant feature, is hidden a third. The relationship of these two developments has been intimate. Although formally independent, they have reacted upon each other through mutual stimulus and enrichment. But the rela-

tionship has not been strictly reciprocal. On the contrary, causal influence has been mainly from *Christian missions* upon *Christian unity*. The Christian world mission has been both precursor and progenitor of the movement for Christian unity.

II

In this chapter, let us attempt first to achieve something of a conspectus, a bird's-eye view, of the world Christian movement today, especially in its outreach across the face of the earth.

What are the concrete realities of the world Christian movement today?

The population of the earth is estimated at 2,800,000,000 persons. Of these, roughly one third (1,000,000,000, that is, 36 per cent) dwell within what used to be (mistakenly) called the Christian world—Europe, North and South America; two thirds (1,800,000,000, i.e., 64 per cent) live in what have traditionally been known as mission lands, i.e., Asia, Africa, Oceania. Today, these are more often and more properly spoken of as, respectively, areas of the older and younger churches.[1]

Among the total of 2,800,000,000, between a quarter and a third have some Christian allegiance; as we have noted, the Christian constituency is about 850,000,000.

Of the Christian grand total of between eight and nine hundred million, well over half dwell in Europe (almost 465,000,000) while only 170,000,000 are credited to North America and almost as many to South America (122,000,000).[2] The number of Chris-

---

[1] The term "younger churches" is not altogether accurate, for example, as applied to India, which embraces some of the most ancient churches of Christendom, e.g., the Syrian Orthodox Church. Nevertheless, this term is widely employed and generally accepted.

[2] The major obstacle to accurate statistical comparisons is here vividly illustrated, e.g., different principles in determining "Christians." Catholics and certain Protestant state churches include all baptized children. Most Protestant churches count only adult church members. This accounts for the relatively high figures for Europe and South America and the low figures for North America. This difficulty plagues the conscientious statistician at almost every point.

tians in so-called non-Christian lands with their population of
1,800,000,000 is estimated as about 82,000,000 (5 per cent of the
total). This is slightly less than one tenth of all the Christians in
the world. Indeed, Christians in all the younger churches number
only half as many as in North America.

Turning now to the proportions of Christians affiliated with
each of the three major divisions of Christendom—Roman Catholic, Eastern Orthodox, and Protestant—the Protestant Christian
community numbers about 250,000,000 among the grand total of
850,000,000 Christians, or roughly 30 per cent. It is peculiarly
difficult to give an accurate figure for adherents of the dozen
Eastern Orthodox communions because of the large measure of
uncertainty regarding what has traditionally been much the
largest and strongest of them—the Church of Russia. If we seek
comparable figures, which must be in terms of all within the
active influence of the respective churches rather than their formal memberships, we are probably not far wrong in thinking of
Roman Catholics as about one half of the over-all total, Protestants another third, and all others (mainly Eastern Orthodox)
about one sixth. But in "lands of the younger churches," Cath-
olicism and Protestantism divide the total of about 80,000,000
almost equally; the missionary activities of Orthodox communions are inconsequential. Therefore, Protestants in younger-
church areas total about 40,000,000 (2½ per cent of the populaces).

In summary, among the total population of the earth, between
one quarter and one third have Christian affinities, divided
among Catholics (55 per cent), Protestants (30 per cent) and
Orthodox (15 per cent). In all younger-church lands, Christians
average only about 5 per cent of the populaces, divided roughly
equally between Catholics and Protestants. This gives us some
conception both of the present extent of Christian affiliation and
of the enormous numbers of mankind as yet unclaimed by Christianity.

They are to be found—these 40,000,000 or so persons of Protestant affiliation in non-Christian lands—in about 100 countries,
in connection with over 6,000 mission (or church) centers.[3] One
should always remember that traditionally a "mission center" has
meant, not just a church or even a church and school and hospi-

3 It must be recalled that the "mission center" is, in many areas, largely a
thing of the past. The figures here given were assembled in 1937.

tal, but an organized unit for a considerable area or even nation.

For example, in 1937 there were in connection with these 6,000 centers, over 55,000 churches and, interestingly enough, a slightly larger number of schools and colleges. There were 62,000 Sunday schools, 3,500 hospitals and dispensaries, and, in addition, a very large number of other adjuncts of the Christian mission that we shall not attempt to enumerate—leprosaria, agricultural institutes, social service centers, publishing houses, etc. All these have their invaluable place in the total enterprise, and no picture of it is adequate that does not constantly bear them in view.

Who actually directed this vast and complex enterprise of Christian service overseas? Over 25,000 ordained ministers, both native and foreign; over 100,000 native teachers (this ratio of considerably more than four to one as between teachers and preachers gives a hint of the place that education holds in the Christian mission); 20,000 doctors and nurses; and about 100,000 other workers—a grand total of just under 250,000 active workers, or an average of over forty for each mission center. Of these, slightly over 25,000, or about 10 per cent, were foreign missionaries;[4] all the others were of the nationality of the native church and among the fruits of its influence.

And the annual cost? Almost exactly $60,000,000,[5] of which only slightly more than half was sent out year by year from the treasuries of the older churches of the West, the remainder being contributed on the field.

Several points hidden within these figures deserve special note in case they have escaped attention:

1. The typical Protestant mission center has consisted of close to ten churches, ten schools, somewhat over ten Sunday schools, and in more than half the instances, a hospital or dispensary, plus other types of institutions. It has been manned by about forty workers, four of them foreigners and thirty-six native members of the church. Probably four of the forty were ordained ministers, another three or four were doctors or nurses, sixteen or seventeen were native teachers, and the others, foreign teachers and workers in a variety of special functions. It ministered to an active con-

[4] The Missionary Research Library has tabulated the total of protestant missionaries in 1960 as 42,257.

[5] The Missionary Research Library reports that in 1960 the total income of North American Foreign Mission Boards alone was $175,885,920.

stituency of about 2,500 persons, of whom 1,000 were actual church members and the others baptized adherents or children in school. They were supported in their tasks by annual expenditures of only $10,000, of which $5,000 was raised in the field of work and $5,000 came to them from Christian friends in other lands. To the latter figure, however, must be added the salaries of the missionary staff who were supported entirely by mission societies of the older churches.

2. As pointed out, each church normally had associated with it a school and one or more Sunday schools. There was a hospital or at least a dispensary for every sixteen churches.

3. The number of native leaders was about four times as great as the number of foreign missionaries.

4. The financial resources came about equally from local contributions and from overseas. Therefore, the native leaders had gone about four times as far in assuming *direction* of their Christian enterprises as in undertaking responsibility for their *support*. Nevertheless, that they could make themselves responsible for almost half the expenses is a statistical indicator of the degree to which the Christian mission had become truly indigenous and of the sound strength of these younger Christian churches.

5. For a complete impression of Christianity at work in these lands, the Protestant figures should be roughly doubled to include Catholic work which at so many points almost parallels that of the Protestant churches.

6. Only about 5 per cent of all persons dwelling in these lands which harbor nearly two thirds of the earth's population are being even touched by Catholic and Protestant churches combined.

The six thousand centers of the Christian world mission on every continent are marked by a most extraordinary *sameness*. This is an unexpected and inescapable impression made upon anyone who travels widely among them. With all its diversity, springing from different origins and adapted to varying situations, the Christian world mission wherever one encounters it is unmistakably one, and not merely in its setting and work but no less in its inner genius. The explanation lies at a deeper level—the source of the whole in one faith rooted in one Lord. There is no other movement that thus encircles the earth and that is thus basically the same everywhere.

This mark of sameness applies not only to geographical distribution. There is a no less obvious similarity whatever the denominational affinity. The divergences among the various Christian communions and between churchmen of different countries are great, are often felt to be vital, and are not to be underestimated. Nevertheless, the fact must be faced that these differences almost wholly escape those who travel in far places of the earth, and their admiration for centers of Christian life and work has no appreciable relation to their denominational bases or to denominational kinship between them and their discoverers.

The reason is at least twofold. For one thing, under the exigencies of pioneering tasks amidst adverse conditions, Christians of all persuasions tend to develop mutual appreciation, to discover their affinities, and to submerge their disagreements.

More important, face to face with the needs of human beings still living in primitive squalor and superstition, or even where the great non-Christian faiths have failed to bring a ministry of healing, enlightenment of mind, emancipation of womankind and credible, compelling faith, Christianity of whatever persuasion stands in such striking contrast to all that surrounds it that the differences of theology and ecclesiastical tradition fade into relative insignificance.

A further impression is of the *comprehensiveness of the Christian program,* and of the soundness of such a full-orbed ministry to human life. If there are those who still harbor the caricature of a Christian missionary as a solitary foreign evangelist exhorting his hearers to forsake their heathen faith and accept his beliefs, such an absurd misconception might well be consigned to the dusty repository of infantile toys and childhood legends. The typical mission is a center of three or four buildings—hospital, school, church—from which a team of co-workers with varied gifts and equipment—minister, doctor, nurse, teacher, social worker, agriculturalist—go forth into the community and its environs in multiform but unified service to all who will accept their help. The Christian mission is still teaching men to worship the Lord their God with all their minds and strength as well as hearts and souls. This *is* the full and authentic Christian gospel. It is also the only program for individual or community that offers promise of true health of body or mind or spirit.

Here is the main point: the glory of the Christian mission is not in this or that piece of exceptional work, or in the work of any one of our multitudinous communions. It is—the *Christian movement* in its entirety, in its whole sweep and reach. It is the

total impact of the Christian movement that is important—an
impact effected by the combined influence of innumerable enterprises and of unnumbered and unnamed individuals, both
nationals and foreigners, who give tirelessly to its tasks their best
ability and devotion.

III

In preparation for the World Missionary Conference at Madras
in 1938, the International Missionary Council published a *Conspectus of Co-operative Missionary Enterprises* prepared by Dr.
Charles H. Fahs and Dr. Helen E. Davis, which ran to some two
hundred and fifty pages. This is much the most comprehensive
tabulation of instances of Christian collaboration that has ever
been assembled. It is regrettable that it was not revised regularly
through the succeeding quarter century and has never been fully
brought down to date so that there is no similar current directory
through which accurate comparisons can be made.

In their General Introduction, the editors of the *Conspectus*
appropriately called attention to the report of Commission VIII
at the Edinburgh World Missionary Conference of 1910 on "Co-
operation and the Promotion of Unity." This was the Edinburgh
Commission that had made bold to sponsor the then daring proposal of "an international committee" to "serve as a medium of
communication" (sic). And it was the Continuation Committee
thus created that eventuated eleven years later in the International Missionary Council, the first permanent organ of world-
wide Christian consultation and, in no small measure, the in-
spiration and model for the later world-wide bodies of church
conference and collaboration. It is interesting to note that the
Edinburgh report had differentiated five forms or levels of Christian co-operation. These were precisely five of the six types into
which we were led to classify the historical data in the preceding
chapter—*comity, conference, joint action, federation,* and *organic union.*

The *Conspectus* of 1934, supplemented by two unpublished
essays, enumerated nearly four hundred "co-operative enter-

prises" functioning at that time either on the mission field or among the missionary agencies of the sending countries. Some of these, to be sure, represented successive steps in single lines of development. A few were relatively inconsequential. Others, though surprisingly few, were interdenominational only in the sense of joining the work of churches of the same communion, for example, Presbyterian and Reformed or different branches of Lutheranism. In 1934, these were considered significant achievements in "interdenominational co-operation" and are included in the tables given here. Such instances of collaboration *within* the same communion are disregarded in all the rest of our discussion. Furthermore, thorough as were their researches, the eyes of the editors of the 1934 *Conspectus* overlooked not a few enterprises, some of them of considerable interest and importance, that should have found places in their tabulations. And careful as were their classifications, they slipped into a number of incongruities; witness the fact that interdenominational theological education—certainly one of the most significant categories—appears in two places in their listings, under both "Higher Education" and "Secondary and Primary Education." Granted these limitations, however, the *Conspectus* supplies a conscientious, invaluable, and impressive bird's-eye view of the world picture of Christian collaboration at that date. The total of undertakings originally classified was 256, of which fifty-four represented joint work merely within denominational families, but by far the larger proportion, 202 in all, were in the fullest sense *inter*denominational. The variety, scope, and extent of Christian co-operation in the mid-thirties is indicated by the tables on the following pages.

CO-OPERATIVE MISSIONARY ENTERPRISES, 1934

5. *Christian Literature* 12
   (Unfortunately, this section of the *Conspectus* made no effort
   to enumerate the many Bible societies, tract societies, Christian
   literature societies, union missions presses, etc., that had
   sprung up in almost every major area, but contented itself
   with descriptions of the then situation in six of these areas.
   The Brown Ecumenical Library *Chronology of Christian Co-
   operation and Union* records the founding of 12 such agencies
   before 1934, but there were doubtless many others.)

6. *Union Churches* 18

   Interdenominational 6
   Denominational* 12
                                                                   ——
                                                                   18

7. *Miscellaneous* 22

   Union 16
   Denominational* 6
                                                                   ——
                                                                   22

   Grand total 256
   Union 202
   Denominational 54
                                                                   ——
                                                                   256

Commenting upon the contrast between the situation revealed
by their own studies of 1934 and that which had confronted the
Edinburgh Conference of 1910, the Editors of the *Conspectus*
remarked:

> In general, during this quarter century co-operation has moved on
> into an entirely new stage—one of greater maturity, of greater scope,
> comprehensiveness and complexity, and a greater degree of accept-
> ance by most of the agencies concerned. . . .
>
> Comity and the principle of division of territory are taken for
> granted now by most boards and their missions. Lesser phases or
> examples of co-operation, which together formed so important a
> part of the Edinburgh picture, are now so numerous, so varied, and
> so widespread in their incidence that only a long catalogue of head-
> ings by types and by geographic areas would suffice to name them
> and to give them their settings. . . .
>
> Conferences have assumed in these later years significance, repre-
> sentative character, and solidity of action to a degree scarcely con-
> templated by the seers of Edinburgh . . . . "Joint Action" has flowered
> amazingly in the last decades.[6]

6 P. 2.

As we have said, no comparable *Conspectus* for 1960 is available. However, compilers of a parallel tabulation for today would be tempted to paraphrase the observation of the editors of 1934 as they sought to compare their task with that of the Commission of Edinburgh, 1910: "Lesser phases and examples of co-operation, which together formed so important a part of the 1934 picture, are now so numerous, so varied, and so widespread in their incidence that only a long catalogue of headings by types and by geographic areas would suffice to name them and to give their settings."

But certain selected comparisons may serve to give us a not unreliable impression of the trends of the past quarter century and of the enlargements and fulfillments of Christian unity achieved. For this purpose, it will be useful to continue the classification of the preceding chapter. Passing over *consultation* and *comity* as no longer sufficiently significant to justify attention and passing over *co-operation* as today much too general and numerous to permit detailed examination, we may focus our attention successively upon *federation, union institutions,* and *church union.*

Christian Councils

The historical review in the preceding chapter disclosed that the modern impulse toward Christian unity found first expression in the joining of Christian *individuals,* not *church officials,* for a more effective discharge of common missionary concern, that the earliest transdenominational meetings of *ecclesiastical representatives* were of mission board secretaries at the home base and of missionaries on the mission field and that these were at the elementary level of consultations, that such consultations gradually evolved into conferences assembling periodically and then annually, that many of these in turn eventually developed into continuing federations or councils, functioning through standing committees and later served by part-time and even full-time staffs, and that the latter anticipated and often became the basis of the national Christian councils and councils of churches of today. And we made note of the phenomenal multiplication of federations and councils during the past half century to the present total of sixty-eight such national bodies, seventeen of them in countries of Europe, North America and Australasia, but fifty-one of them within the lands of the younger churches of Africa, Asia, and Latin America.

The entire Christian-unity development of the last century and a half, we have pointed out, is a phenomenon without precedent and without anticipation in the previous eighteen centuries of Christian history. This overarching fact has somewhat overshadowed one of its more recent specific features that, in later perspective, may come to be recognized as its most novel and most significant achievement—the appearance within Christendom of the Christian council and council of churches. For if the larger trend toward interdenominational fellowship, association, and co-operation is without precedent and without anticipation in Christian history, no less is the modern council without precedent and without anticipation in the life of the church of Christ across the ages.

We must not be misled by the similarity of name to the so-called ecumenical councils of the early centuries. In no significant sense were they analogous to, or forerunners of, the councils of churches of today. They were occasional assemblages of groups of bishops, seldom adequately representative of the whole of Christendom of that day, who came together to wrestle with specific current issues, usually conflict over heresy or ecclesiastical authority. In our nomenclature, they were "conferences" not "councils." Viewed through the rose-tinted lenses of distance and idealization, they have been invested by tradition with an aura of wisdom and authority that careful historical inquiry cannot validate. In comparison with the World Council of Churches, for example, all of them, with the possible exception of the earliest at Nicaea in 325, give the impression of predominantly sectional or regional conclaves of embattled ecclesiastics engaged in ineffectual efforts to secure or maintain theological uniformity and thus heal divisions or avert schisms. In these purposes they were singularly unsuccessful.[7] Apart from their partial representativeness and limited objectives, the main point is that they contemplated and provided no continuing instrumentalities for consultation, let alone for united action.

In contrast, the Christian council of today, whether within a nation or on a world scale, is a permanent organ of officially designated representatives of its member bodies authorized within prescribed limits not only to speak but to act in their behalf in the discharge of mutually accepted responsibilities in obedience to the one Lord of the church. Its controlling objective is the

[7] Compare Henry P. Van Dusen, *World Christianity: Yesterday, Today, and Tomorrow* (Abingdon Press, 1947), pp. 71 ff.

more faithful proclamation of Christ's gospel and the more effective furtherance of his purposes. The Christian council is something genuinely *new*, a new form of the body of Christ furnished with new organs of its life, which the Spirit of Christ has brought into existence and is nurturing to maturity and increasing fruitfulness in our own day. Thus is taking place under our eyes what may safely be identified as one of the most important as well as original developments within the Christian church of all time. The theological significance of what has already taken place and is continuing to take place has hardly begun to be explored. We shall return to this later.[8]

It must be recognized that these sixty-six Christian councils are far from uniform. They vary enormously in their constituencies, in the scope of their objectives and the scale of their operations, in the effectiveness of their organizations and programs.

Some are scarcely more than continuing conferences, with annual meetings for consultation and without benefit of regular staffs or adequate resources. Others, national and local as well as world councils, are highly developed organizations, with wide-ranging programs, substantial budgets, and considerable full-time leadership.

Some of the Christian councils set forth detailed creedal statements to which adherence is required. Many of them do not. Some affirm the brief *Basis* of the World Council of Churches or the *Purpose* of the International Missionary Council. Scattered as they are on six continents, it is doubtful how great has been the mutual stimulus and suggestion in the formulation of aims. And yet there are striking parallels that spring rather from inherent identity of purpose than from any conscious effort after uniformity—strong unintended witness to the basic unity within this widespread movement of "conciliar ecumenicity."

Many declare, as their first objective: "to proclaim and maintain Evangelical Christianity," or "to promote the extension of the Kingdom of God among all races." A number still acknowledge the task "to preserve comity among churches and missions." Almost all aim "to co-ordinate Christian forces (or the work of member churches) for a more effective propagation of the gospel." Most of them are authorized "to carry on co-operative undertakings" or "to take joint action" especially in social, moral, religious, and educational matters. Several of the councils

8 See Part III, pp. 127 ff.

on the African Continent are charged "to represent Christian forces in relation to government" or "to speak on behalf of the churches in dealing with government," some "to guard freedom to preach the gospel," others "to help form enlightened Christian public opinion." A number declare their concern "to develop spiritual life." But the note struck by all of them, although with variations of phrase and emphasis, is the advance of Christian unity and church union: "to foster fellowship and unity and develop ecumenical consciousness," "to further fellowship and the unity of the church," "to develop the sense of one church among all Christians," "to show the unity of Protestant churches and their communion with the universal church," or "to express unitedly in visible form the unity of the church in order to bear more effective witness to Christ." One of the most succinct comprehensive statements (Sierra Leone United Christian Council) is: "to restore the unity of the church of Christ, preserve comity among the churches, serve as spokesman of the church on religious, educational, moral, social, and other matters, . . . and to take joint action." Representative of the outlook, presuppositions, and purposes that animate most of them is this brief declaration of the Philippine Federation of Christian Churches:

> Believing in the essential unity of the Christian churches and desiring to bring about closer relationship among them and to foster their unity to secure effective results in efforts to win men to fuller life in Jesus Christ, the Federation seeks to provide a channel for Christian fellowship and promote more effective understanding and co-operation in the work of various Christian bodies with the aim of bringing them ultimately to organic union.

With all their kinship of purpose and similarity in methods for its realization, there are two important and closely related respects in which these councils reveal wide differences—in the comprehensiveness of their constituencies and in their relationships to the world ecumenical bodies.

As might be expected, the major historic Protestant Communions that are members of the World Council of Churches are generally represented within the memberships of national councils and councils of churches everywhere. But as fellow members of Christian councils among the younger churches are also to be found groups that thus far have held aloof from the World Council—Adventist, Holiness, Pentecostal, and various individual missions and churches of strongly conservative outlook and allegiance—although in varying numbers and strength in different areas. For example, the Congo Protestant Council, the earliest major council in Africa dating from 1924, embraces in addition to Anglicans, Baptists, Disciples of Christ, Lutherans, Mennonites, Methodists, and Presbyterians, the following: Berean African Missionary Society, Congo Evangelistic Mission, North Sankuru Mission, Congo Gospel Mission, Congo Inland Mission, Christian and Missionary Alliance, Heart of Africa Mission, Africa Evangelistic Band, Assemblies of God, Pentecostals, World Gospel Mission, Worldwide Grace Testimony, Africa Inland Mission, Unevangelized Fields Mission, and others. And the youngest council in Latin America, that of Bolivia founded in 1955, includes in its membership the New Testament Missionary Union, Assemblies of God, Church of God (Holiness), Church of the Nazarene, International Church of the Four Square Gospel, Bethesda Bolivian Mission, Evangelical Union of South America, World Mission Prayer League, Methodist Holiness, and International Child Evangelism Fellowship, as well as representatives of the Baptist, Brethren, Friends, and Methodist Communions.

The bearing of this diversity in constituencies upon the relations of national Christian councils to the world ecumenical bodies is direct and of utmost importance. The active particpation of some of the missions and groups that incline toward calling themselves Evangelicals has prevented a number of the councils from affiliating with the International Missionary Council. It was the influence of these groups that led the Congo Protestant Council, the original member council from Africa, to withdraw from the International Missionary Council in 1958 when the latter's integration with the World Council of Churches appeared assured. Many, though by no means all, of the missions, churches, and groups that stand apart from these two world bodies find their wider association within the world evangelical fellowship.

The upshot of this fact to which we are calling attention is that while in Asia most national Christian councils are constituent members of the International Missionary Council (eleven out of thirteen) and a number of them (four out of thirteen) are associated with the World Council of Churches, in Africa such affiliation is exceptional and in Latin America far from usual. Of the seventeen full councils in Africa, only seven have taken their places in the International Missionary Council; none has sought association with the World Council. Of the eighteen councils in Latin America, just half are within the International Missionary Council; only one is associated with the World Council.

On the other hand, these relationships are by no means a simple question of co-operation or non-co-operation. For example, the Federation of Protestant Churches of the Argentine, one of the oldest and strongest member bodies of the International Missionary Council in South America, embraces the Christian and Missionary Alliance, Evangelical Church "Grace and Glory," Church of the Nazarene, Evangelical Pentecostal Church, "Emanuel" Evangelical Mission, Church of God, and Union of the Christians of the Evangelical Faith (Pentecostal). And the Division of Foreign Missions of the National Council of Churches U.S.A., the largest and certainly one of the most influential member churches of the World Council of Churches, includes among its member boards and societies the Seventh Day Baptists, Churches of God, Evangelical Covenant Church and Congo Inland Mission, among its Associated Boards the Advent Christian Church, Seventh-day Adventists, Church of God, Lutheran Church—Missouri Synod, and Assemblies of God, and as a Related Agency, the United Free Gospel and Missionary Society.

The import of these facts for the future of the entire ecumenical development can hardly be exaggerated. It presents the World Council and the International Missionary Council on the eve of their integration into a more comprehensive World Council of Churches with perhaps their most baffling and urgent problem—their future relations with dynamic, widely dispersed, and rapidly multiplying groups that are presently outside their ecumenical fellowship. To this issue we shall return as we attempt to look at the major issues for ecumenical Christianity in the days immediately ahead.[9]

No consideration of Christian councils however summary would be complete without reference to still another type of such councils that stands intermediate between national and world bodies—the regional Christian conference or council. In recommending integration of the World Council of Churches and the International Missionary Council, the Joint Committee of the two bodies called attention to "the emergence of a dynamic regionalism in the world of our time—the feeling of peoples in

9 See Part III, pp. 146 ff.

great areas of the globe that they belong together and are involved in a common destiny."

As a matter of fact, regionalism is not a wholly new factor in the ecumenical development. Since 1927, missions and churches of the Eastern Mediterranean have been linked in the Near East Christian Council, which now embraces—in addition to thirteen churches and thirteen missions—four subsidiary regional councils: those of Iran, Egypt, North Sudan, and Southwest Asia. The Evangelical Confederation of the River Plate in South America antedated and now embraces federations of Protestant churches of the Argentine, Paraguay, and Uruguay. The Protestant Alliance in Ruanda-Urundi is affiliated with the Congo Protestant Council. And most of the member missions of the Christian Council of Mozambique also hold membership in the Christian Council of South Africa.

The dynamic regionalism to which the Joint Committee was calling special attention is, however, of more recent date and wider radius. It is illustrated by the coming into being in 1959 of the East Asia Christian Conference, which is structurally and functionally in the fullest sense a Regional Council, the All-Africa Church Conference of 1958, which seems likely to develop along somewhat similar lines into a continuing regional body, and the possibility of similar developments in South America and perhaps elsewhere. The Joint Committee went on to point out that "churches and councils in different regions are in different stages of development and have differing perspectives with regard to the ecumenical ideal. The needs and developments within the regions themselves must determine the pattern of the ecumenical service given and received." The wisdom of this last injunction has led the world ecumenical bodies to refrain from any attempt to influence the direction that regional developments may take but, rather, to encourage the maximum of indigenous spontaneity. Unquestionably, this may make for greater divergences among regional organizations than prevails among national councils, with resulting confusion in the larger ecumenical scene. But this is regarded as an inescapable corollary of full autonomy. It may also result in diverse patterns of relationship of regional to world ecumenical bodies. The East Asia Christian Conference owes its existence very largely to the services rendered to the churches of that vast area by the Joint East Asia Secretariat of the International Missionary Council and the

World Council of Churches. And it has continued in a free but thus far loosely defined relationship to the two world bodies. Doubtless something of the same sort will be the natural evolution as other regional structures take shape. More than that at this stage no one can safely forecast. It can be said, however, that such regional developments are among the most vital and promising as well as unpredictable facts of contemporary ecumenical Christianity.

Union Institutions—Theological Education

Our earlier study fastened upon one "particular type of union institution that has exerted the largest influence upon the overall advance of Christian unity." This is the interdenominational theological school.[10]

It might be expected that theological education would have been one of the last areas of missionary work to come under the influence of Christian co-operation. The preparation of the church's professional leadership is usually the last redoubt of denominational particularism. So it was that union institutions for both higher and secondary general education, for medical and teacher training, as well as for the production and distribution of Christian literature of all kinds long antedated nondenominational training of the ministry. The two earliest union theological seminaries were founded in the same year—1907—in Manila by Presbyterians and Methodists, later joined by United Brethren and Congregationalists, and in Indore, Central India. Be it noted, this was one year before the first church federation of major rank (the American Federal Council) and before the first instance of church union across denominational lines, in South India, both in 1908. But it was more than half a century after similar schools had been launched in the West.

The late initiation of interdenominational theological training was to be expected. What was hardly to be anticipated was its rapid multiplication. It is probably not an exaggeration that today theological education is the area of life of the younger churches in which co-operation is both most general and most advanced.

The Theological Education Fund of the International Missionary Council, building upon Mr. Yorke Allen's massive detailed and authoritative inquiry into training for the ministry

10 See Part I, pp. 42 ff.

among the younger churches of all Christian communions,[11] has prepared a comprehensive enumeration of "Theological Schools in Africa, Asia, the Caribbean, Latin America, and the Southwest Pacific" as of June 1960. It lists a total of 232. Of these, no fewer than sixty-eight or more than one fourth are "union" institutions. Needless to say, this is a far higher proportion than would be found within the areas of the older churches of Europe and North America. Twelve of the sixty-eight are "union" because they are training schools for united churches; three are within Government institutions; fifty-three are in the literal sense "interdenominational."

The total number of students for ordination in the 232 schools is 7,109, an average of slightly over thirty per school. Of these students 2,429 or some 35 per cent are being trained in union institutions that have an average student body of just over thirty-six. The 232 schools report over-all staffs of 1,937 teachers, 1,065 on full time and 872 on part time (respectively 4.6 and 3.8 or a total of 8.4 per school), with an average teacher-student ratio of about one to seven full time and one to eight part time or a total of more than one instructor for every four students—an almost fantastically favorable ratio according to standards of traditional theological education in the West. In the sixty-seven union institutions, the total teaching staffs number 710, 393 on full time and 317 on part time (respectively 5.9 and 4.7 or a total of 10.6 per institution), with an average teacher-student ratio of about one to six full time and one to eight part time or a total of better than one instructor for every four students. In summary, nearly one third of all younger church training schools for their ministries are nondenominational; they are preparing more than one third of all candidates; they are provided with somewhat larger teaching staffs and maintain a slightly better proportion of teachers to students.

They are widely scattered across the world, these sixty-eight interdenominational or nondenominational training schools for the leadership of the churches of tomorrow—in Asia, 39; in Africa, 20; in Latin America, 7; in the Near East, 2. As might be anticipated, India leads with 21 of the 34 seminaries in that land;

---

11 Yorke Allen, Jr., *A Seminary Survey* (Harper & Brothers, 1960), pp. 640. The Missionary Research Library issued in 1960 an even more comprehensive, inclusive, and accurate *Directory of Protestant Theological Seminaries and Bible Schools in Asia, the Middle East, Latin America, the Caribbean, and Pacific Areas.*

then follow Japan with 6 out of 13; Nigeria and South Africa with 4 each; the Philippines, 3; Indonesia and Ghana and Korea and Jamaica, 2 each.

Some of the union schools are, to be sure, at the most elementary of the three levels of theological training that were differentiated in the definitive report of the Madras Conference of 1938 on "The Indigenous Ministry of the Church, Both Ordained and Lay"[12]—that of Bible schools which presuppose only secondary or primary school preparation or its equivalent for admission. But over fifty are to be classified at the two higher levels —theological schools, the standard of entrance to which is ordinarily the same as that of matriculation in a university, or theological colleges, which require for admission, as is the normative standard among the older churches, a college degree in arts or science. Indeed, of the twenty-eight schools that require a college degree or its equivalent for admission, just one half, fourteen, are interdenominational whereas, as we observed above, the number of union institutions is less than one third of the total. In contrast, of the sixty schools that admit students with only primary education, only seven are interdenominational while fifty-three are denominational.

In the markedly higher requirements for admission to the nondenominational schools is implied the most important single fact. As always, numbers are less significant than quality. It is precisely here that the contrast is most arresting and both little known and little appreciated among the older churches. The roll of the foremost theological seminaries of the younger churches is composed almost altogether of nondenominational institutions— the Union Theological Seminary, Tokyo, and the School of Theology of the Doshisha University in Japan; Union Seminary, Manila, and the School of Theology of Silliman University in the Philippines; all the strongest institutions in China; Trinity College, Singapore; Bangalore and Serampore and Leonard in India; the Near East School of Theology at Beirut; the Protestant Seminaries in Buenos Aires, Havana, San Juan, Mexico City, and Kingston, in the Western Hemisphere; and a growing number of the most promising training colleges in Africa. It is hardly too much to say that, with relatively few notable exceptions (Tainan Theological Seminary, perhaps two or three of the stronger Anglican or Lutheran schools), every theological seminary of front rank among the younger churches is a

12 *The World Mission of the Church,* pp. 66 ff.

union institution. Here is the main point: throughout the areas
of the younger churches, interdenominational or nondenominational theological education is increasingly the prevailing pattern.
Among institutions of the highest standing, it is well-nigh universal.

To be sure, these union institutions do not always include all
Christian communions in their areas. Generally speaking, Lutherans maintain their own seminaries and insist that their leaders
be trained in them. Anglicans often hold to a parallel line,
though by no means always; Anglicans are active participants in
twenty-two of the sixty-eight centers of united theological education in India, Korea, Singapore, Ghana, Kenya, Nigeria, the Sudan, Liberia, South Africa, and Cuba. Nevertheless, the prevailing apartness of these two great communions, as also of churches
stemming from the American Southern Baptist and other separa-
tist groups, in the preparation of their ministries may carry, im-
plicity though not consciously or intentionally, consequences of
gravest import for the entire enterprise of *Christian unity* in the
period ahead, and not among the younger churches only. As nondenominational theological training becomes increasingly the
normal and usual experience of ministers of all Protestant communions *except* Anglican and Lutheran and some Baptist, as it
so generally is even now in younger church lands, is it not more
than likely that a coalescence of outlook and conviction will
grow, that those so trained will come to acknowledge their kinship within a common allegiance, that every type of Christian
co-operation between churches of their allegiance, even Church
union, will speed forward? In consequence, the most significant
alignment within the ecumenical fellowship may tend to become
between those who have and those who have not learned the
reality of *Christian unity* in both conviction and experience during the crucially formative years of ministerial training, that is,
between Lutherans and Anglicans on the one hand, and almost
all the rest of ecumenical Protestantism on the other. In the
measure that some such development occurs, we would confront
an altered ecumenical situation. "Most unfortunate," many
would regard such a new and sharp alignment between the two
great liturgical communions and all others. Yes, doubtless, in
many ways. But if the obverse of its disadvantages should prove
to be steady advance of non-Anglican-Lutheran Christians into
deeper understanding, mounting respect, wider fellowship, fuller
and fuller collaboration, and even organic church union, should

not the development be entered on the credit side of the Christian unity ledger?

It is not sufficiently recognized that nondenominational theological education need not follow a single, uniform pattern. On the contrary, there are at least four principal alternative plans, one or two of which deserve fuller exploration and trial:

1. When the term "Union Theological Seminary" is spoken, probably the picture that comes most readily to mind is that of one or another of the foremost theological schools in America— for example, the one in New York which bears that name. It should be clearly recognized that schools of this type are *not*, strictly speaking, *inter*denominational at all, but rather *non*denominational. They are independent and responsible to no particular ecclesiastical body. There is, I believe, no instance of this type of *non*denominational seminary among the younger churches except divinity schools attached to Government universities.

2. The truly *inter*denominational school might, more properly, be termed a "united theological college," as is the case with one of the most representative leaders, at Bangalore in India. Here, the institution is maintained by several different denominations that contribute their resources of staff and money, however, to a completely unified faculty, program, and budget. Most of the union theological seminaries of the younger churches follow this general pattern, e.g., in Tokyo, Manila, Beirut, Buenos Aires, etc.

3. Still another possibility differs from the one just described in that denominational hostels are provided for students of the co-operating communions in order that they may live and, possibly, worship apart. There may also be a minimum number of courses (in church polity, liturgics, etc.) offered for students of the several communions separately, and perhaps taught in connection with their life and worship together in their denominational hostels. Speaking of a desirable collaboration of two theological schools in Ghana—one a joint Methodist and Presbyterian enterprise, the other of Anglo-Catholic cast—Bishop Neill suggested: "It might be possible to plan for the coexistence within a single college of two hostels, with considerable independence in matters of devotion and discipline, but with a common faculty and much teaching in common."[13]

13 Stephen Neill, *Survey of the Training of the Ministry in Africa* (International Missionary Council, 1950–1954), Part I, p. 52.

4. Finally, there is the pattern in which the several participating denominations maintain legally autonomous institutions, but in the closest possible geographic propinquity and fellowship, with greater or lesser measure of integration of their educational programs. Referring to the situation in Ghana, Bishop Neill proffered an alternative to his suggestion outlined just above: "The coexistence on adjacent sites of two colleges, entirely independent in organization, but with much closer fellowship and more exchange of teaching than is possible at present."[14] This would be an instance of federated theological schools. It opens up endless possibilities of variation and experimentation.

Lastly, how comes it that interdenominational theological education has gone so far in the lands of the younger churches, so very much farther and faster than anywhere in the West? Two factors appear to have been mainly influential.

In part, interdenominational co-operation in training of the ministry is a direct consequence of limitations in resources. The bald truth is that there is almost nowhere among the younger churches where a single denomination can afford to deploy sufficient personnel and financial support to maintain a first-rate theological seminary; hence, the plethora of third- and fourth-rate denominational schools. If it is suggested that limitation in resources is a factor of expediency, let thoughtful Christians hesitate to disdain the outcome on that account. They stand within a tradition that recognizes that God can use all manner of very practical and unspiritual instrumentalities, even pagan kings, to further his purposes. And they are heirs of a history that shows countless illustrations of how God has in fact caused even the wrath of man, not to speak of the poverty of men, to praise him.

The major explanation of the prevalence of interdenominational theological education among the younger churches, however, is not deference to the necessities of expediency. It is that underlying factor which we have discovered at every crucial point—profound conviction of the sin of Christian division and desire to effect a larger *Christian unity*. If proof of this were needed, it could be found in the fact that, as resources for separate theological training have grown, the number and strength and inclusiveness of united theological schools have increased. Some of them are, of course, children of union churches. Others have been major influences in bringing union churches to birth.

14 *Ibid.*, p. 53.

Thus, through coalescence of considerations of practical necessity and commands of fundamental principle, the cause of *Christian unity* is furthered. It is the same combination that God has
so often employed for the purposes of his Kingdom. When the
definitive history of *Christian unity* is written, it may appear that
no other single factor was so determinative in the long-time advance as God's use of these two complementary considerations to
bring the oncoming leadership of so many of the churches of
Christ into understanding and fellowship, into profound Christian unity of both conviction and experience through united
preparation for their ministries.

Indigenous Theology

More is at stake in the future of interdenominational theological education in the younger churches than its influence upon
Christian unity, great as that may be. And more is involved in
the program of theological training in the younger churches than
that they should be increasingly ecumenical, important as that is.
What shall be the *content* of that education? And what may
union institutions contribute to the development of an *ecumenical theology?* The question here raised is that of so-called indigenous theology.

It has long been recognized that the most retarded aspect of
the life of the younger churches is in the interpretation of Christian faith in terms of Christian theology. Two decades ago, on
the basis of visits to younger church areas throughout Asia and
in the perspective of the Madras World Missionary Conference, I
ventured the judgment:

> In one respect only, as it seems to me, indigenization has not yet
> advanced as far as one would wish—in the intellectual interpretation
> of Christian faith, that is to say, in the realm of Christian theology.
> This is not surprising. The energies of the younger churches have
> been preoccupied and are still preoccupied with immediate and prac-
> tical tasks, and rightly so. They have not yet discovered the leisure
> for extensive research and speculation. Their intellectual leaders are
> required for active and general teaching; they cannot be spared
> for the more privileged luxury of cloistered scholarship. Then too,
> Christian theological discussion is prevailingly carried on in Western
> languages (German, French, English) unfamiliar to Eastern speech,
> and in thought forms and presuppositions uncongenial to Oriental
> minds. Moreover, there is no area where familiarity and experience
> rear awesome authority quite so impressively as in intellectual matters.
> It is quite natural that thinkers amongst the younger churches tend

to bow in questions of doctrine before the more mature confidence
of colleagues from the older churches. Furthermore, the natural diffi-
dence of Oriental countesy hesitates to plunge into the arena of theological debate. The result is that Asiatic and African and Latin-
American apprehensions of Christian faith, while very real and
distinctive, have not yet learned to articulate themselves in "indigenous" terms with the fullness, cogency, and logical coherence of
theologies with nineteen centuries of continuous development behind
them.

This is all the more regrettable, however, because Christians of the
younger churches have not only a distinctive but an invaluable contribution to make to the theology of the World Church.[15]

On the other hand, the possibilities of an indigenous theology
among the younger churches, and the urgency that that theology
should someday begin to take form, have long been recognized.
These expectations echo through the speeches of some of the
most prophetic among the earlier missionary leaders.

Evidence is strong that the hour is approaching when original
interpretations of Christian faith not only in the language and
thought forms of younger churchmen but as articulations of their
distinctive apprehensions of that faith, perhaps sharply contrasted
at many points with those familiar to the churches of the West
and the heritage of which they are heirs, will be forthcoming.[16]

It would not be surprising if here, again, India should emerge
as the leader, both because of the relative maturity of Indian
Christianity and because of its long-time interest in the rendering
of Christian truth in relation to the rich, variegated, and lively
philosophical and theological thought of that nation. Indeed, a
promising beginning has been made. Since 1940, under the auspices of the National Christian Council, the ablest Christian
thinkers of India, both missionary and national, have been engaged in a united inquiry into "The Theological Task in India."
A notable Theological Conference at Poona in December, 1942,
outlined the issues. The Rev. Marcus Ward, who had a central

[15] Henry P. Van Dusen, *For the Healing of the Nations* (Charles Scribner's
Sons, 1940), p. 182.

[16] Compare the notable essays by Dean T. C. Chao of China and President
David G. Moses of India in the post-Madras volume, *The Authority of the
Faith,* International Missionary Council, 1939. Dr. Carl Michalson, Professor
of Systematic Theology at Drew University, has recently published a volume
entitled *Japanese Contributions to Christian Theology* (The Westminster
Press, 1960).

place in this undertaking from the outset, thus summarized its consensus:

First, there was no real difference of opinion, in a group representing many traditions and backgrounds, as to the fact that there is a fundamental and unchangeable core of the Christian faith. All agreed that the first concern of Christian theology is with what God has given to, and done for, man. All Christians, whatever their race or communion, have a common heritage which may not be changed or augmented. I do not suggest that there was any agreement as to the nature or substance of this central core, but there was the common conviction that such does exist and that the understanding of its meaning and content is the primary business of theological study.

Secondly, it was agreed that it is our task to interpret the unchanging given gospel in a form sympathetic to, and commanding the assent of, the mind and heart of India. This means, moreover, that Christian India has a charge to keep in bringing her own national inheritance to the understanding and proclamation of the gospel that she, and the whole church of God with her, may thereby be enriched.[17]

The Poona Conference formulated its findings as follows:

We affirm as a guiding principle that the essential content of the Christian faith is the same for all times, places, and circumstances; but that in different times, places, and circumstances the expression, interpretation, and application must both grow out of, and meet, the actual situation, making such particular emphases as are called for.

Hence, within theology, the primary term covering the whole, we distinguish two elements, each of which has its own specific task: (A) The absolute element—the central core—the word of God—DOGMA. (B) The relative element—the expression, interpretation, application—DOCTRINE.

[Here follows a summary of essential DOGMA, God's revelation of himself "in an Act—in Jesus Christ—by which the world has been redeemed."]

(B)

All living Christian doctrine grows out of, and cannot be understood apart from, the worshiping Christian community. And both doctrine and worship presuppose Christian experience, i.e., the corporate conviction of heart and mind that a great event has happened. Here it is our task to interpret the great Act of God in all its bearings; to build implications of the revelation in Christ into a system of thought—reasonable, not in the sense of being demonstrable by argument, but in that it, as does nothing else, makes sense of all the facts.

[17] Marcus Ward, *Our Theological Task*, Christian Literature Society for India, 1946, Preface, p. ix.

This involves clear discernment of our actual situation as Christians, both within the church and facing the needs and circumstances of India.

Each age has its own problems; and in different ages men have arisen who have so handled the needs and forces of their own time as to create a living synthesis, which has not only satisfied contemporary requirements but, when the conditions which produced it are no more, still remains a classic expression from which succeeding generations may learn. We shall do well to remember that such an inheritance is part of our actual situation. Although we have to consider the dogma in the setting of our own world, yet we may seek guidance from those who, facing similar tasks in their own generation, have so carried out the work of an interpretation as to do justice to the real issues.

In brief, therefore, we see it our task: (a) to appropriate dogma— that given, permanent living core, which must determine the characteristic shape of any expression or application which is to be recognizably Christian; (b) to explicate doctrine—on the one hand, for building up Christians and on the other, for presenting the gospel to others. Here we would stress our opinion that the "Indianization" of Christianity refers only to such changes in external forms and terms as will make the unchanging gospel intelligible in India.[18]

Marcus Ward was asked to undertake an explication of these findings that might advance further corporate inquiry. He has done so in a volume, *Our Theological Task,* which has been widely and rightly hailed as marking a fresh beginning in the restatement of Christian faith in Indian terms. With all its value, it is regrettable that this task could not have been undertaken by an Indian Christian, for not until the Indian Christian mind sets itself to expound the faith in its own language and in terms of its own apprehensions will we begin to get what is needed. In the meantime, the corporate inquiry in India goes forward.

In the articulation of indigenous Christian theology, there is an underlying issue of the highest consequence for the whole Christian world. It can be made concrete most clearly in terms of theological education.

No one speaks in this area from wider knowledge or with greater competence than Bishop Stephen Neill, a graduate with highest honors from Cambridge University, deeply and thoroughly schooled in classic Christian theological study, an outstandingly effective teacher of theology in India, Chairman of the justly

18 *Ibid.,* pp. 1–3.

famed Section of the Madras Conference on "The Training of an Indigenous Ministry." Bishop Neill has supplemented his classical Christian theological education and practical experience as theological educator and church administrator in India by a wide-ranging study of theological education in British Africa. Against the immediate background of the latter inquiry, he poses the issue in these words:

> Those who have been studying the subject have concluded that Hebrew modes of thought are much more likely to be congenial to the African than Greek, and that his understanding can link itself much more directly to the Bible itself than to the Western accretions of interpretation that have become so much part of the Western stock in trade that we often confuse them with the Bible itself. It is exceedingly difficult for the Western Christian to realize the extent to which the Greeks still rule the Western world—through Plato and Aristotle and their disciples, through Athanasius and the great creeds and councils, through Augustine and the other Latin fathers who had learned so much from the Greeks.
>
> Is it right that the African mind should be at once made subject to this whole weight of tradition, so little native to its own way of thought? Or would it be wrong to deprive the African student, even for a little time, of what has been found so indispensable to the development of Christian life and experience in the Western world? Should a theological course for the African take its start from the Bible, in its Semitic context, with its dramatic, pictorial, realist form of expression, and bring in the Greeks only at the end of the course, after the African student has fully absorbed the Biblical revelation directly and not through the distorting medium of Hellenism?[19]

With respect to the teaching of church history, he adds:

> The teaching of church history is another point at which the dominantly Western character of syllabuses is manifest. In so far as the subject is taught at all, it tends to concentrate on three epochs— the early church, the period of the Reformation, and the nineteenth century, with special reference to the missionary expansion of the church. But in fact, in the early period the main interest of Western textbooks is in doctrine and heresies, and in the final formulation, under the influence of Hellenic thought, of the classic doctrines of the church. It is natural that churches sprung from the Reformation should regard the period of their own rebirth as of cardinal importance. It is desirable that African ministers should have an understanding of the real differences between the Roman Catholic and the

19 Neill, *op. cit.,* p. 23.

non-Roman forms of the Christian faith, which coexist in all the territories under review. But is an intimate acquaintance with the tortuous history of the Reformation period really necessary for them? Is it not a *reductio ad absurdum,* when African Anglicans are condemned to master in detail the stages by which *The Book of Common Prayer* reached its present form?

What do we really want our African students to learn from the history of the church? What parts of it are really relevant to them at their present stage of development? I could not but feel profound sympathy with the African student who remarked, "It seems to me that missionaries are much too hard in their judgments on the African churches. Did you never have a period of struggle in your own countries?" Indeed we did. In that moment I suddenly saw that, for the African churches in their contemporary struggle, the most important period is the one that ordinarily we never teach them in detail, the Dark Ages. Alcuin, the Venerable Bede, Saint Boniface, the foundation of Cluny—these are the things that would be really illuminating to them as they wrestle with precisely the same difficulties, and are called to find anew the way out of the twilight of the coexistence of old and new into a more genuinely Christian life and social order.[20]

Another English scholar with exceptional qualifications and discerning judgment, Dr. J. W. Welch, the first head of a newly created Department of Religious Studies at the Government University at Ibadan in Nigeria, raised essentially the same query from his practical experience of teaching in one of the most advanced institutions in tropical Africa:

> Classical Christian theology is the child of the marriage between Hebrew religion and Greek philosophy. To Hebrew religion, God was Righteous Will. To Greek philosophy, God was Supreme Intelligence. In A.D. 70 the young Christian church was largely cut off from its Hebraic parent by the fall of Jerusalem; and, at the same time, Christianity moved into a Europe dominated by the ideas of Greek philosophy, Hellenic culture, Roman law and government, and pagan sacrificial cults. . . .
>
> It is legitimate, even for Western Christians, to regret that the influences playing on Christianity during its formative period derived more from Greece than from Palestine. The Western Catholicism we know was largely shaped, in its intellectual formulations, by men trained in Greek philosophy, either in the Platonism of early scholars such as Augustine, or the Aristotelianism of later scholars

20 *Ibid.,* p. 25.

such as Aquinas. Palestinian Christianity in Europe increasingly assumed Greek dress.

The question before African Christians is this: Must African students study Christian theology in its Western, i.e., largely Greek, form, or is the African mind and feeling for religion closer to the Hebraic? And, if so, ought theological teaching in Africa to devote itself to Biblical, largely Hebraic, theology, and to leave the church in Africa to work out its own African formulations of the Christian faith?[21]

Turning to the influence of Western social experience upon Christian theology, Dr. Welch continues:

> In many ways European secular society is the antithesis of the African's society and culture: where ours is materialistic, his is spiritual; where ours is individualistic, his is corporate; where we live in an atomised society, the African is molded by a natural community of family and clan.
>
> These differences help to explain, among many other things, the African love of the Old Testament. The Old Testament, we must remember, is composed almost entirely of books which were written before the influence of Hellenism was felt. . . . The African loves the Old Testament not merely because African society and values are akin to Hebraic society and values. The African understands, better than Europeans, Hebrew religion and social organization; he knows that he is his brother's keeper; he knows what wisdom is even if he is ignorant of our logic; and he does not need abstract Greek ideas to prove the existence of God when the supernatural is as real to him as the material.[22]

Bringing these considerations to focus upon the task of theological education in Africa, Professor Welch asks:

> . . . whether theological education in Africa should follow the Graeco-Christian path of Europe, or whether it should, while avoiding the danger of a false antithesis between the Hebrew and Hellenic elements in Christianity, concentrate as much as possible on the Hebraic-Christian legacy of early Christianity, and leave Africans to make their own formulations of the revelation originally given in Palestine.[23]

Bishop Neill's and Dr. Welch's remarks have the current situation in Africa as their background. They could be made with

[21] James Welch, *Religious Studies in an African University* (Ibadan University Press, Ibadan, Nigeria, 1950), pp. 16–17.
[22] *Ibid.,* p. 18.
[23] *Ibid.,* p. 21.

almost equal relevance in most other younger-church areas, perhaps with even greater weight in areas of most mature culture,
both non-Christian and Christian. The issues they raise are of the
most fundamental and far-reaching character. Immediately, there
is the practical question whether it is necessary for the new Christian, coming directly out of an Oriental or African background
in striking contrast to that of Western Christianity, to be embroiled in the long, tortuous, and often boring route of the pil-
grimage of the Western Christian mind toward the classic formulations of its faith. But behind this immediate and practical issue
are two others, much more searching and radical. One concerns
the Western Christian mind; the other, the Asian and African
Christian mind.

The first is the question how far the classic theology of the
Western churches represents an authentic, definitive, and necessary formulation of basic Christian faith; how far it represents,
rather, a rendering of that faith into the thought forms and in
terms of the intellectual presuppositions of the Greek and modern
European philosophical minds.

The second is the query whether the Asian or African Christian mind—the first because it is Oriental, the second because it
is intuitive, concrete, and nonspeculative—may not be inherently
far better equipped to understand the Bible and thus to appre-
hend essential Christian truth than is possible for the Western
mind, whether ancient or modern.

That this is the insight, not only of Britishers in Africa, but
also of Dutch theologians in Indonesia is suggested by a conversation I had more than two decades ago with the head of the remarkable theological seminary in Batavia (now Jakarta):

> We sat for some time discussing technical problems of theological
> training. . . . Eventually our talk inevitably veered to theology, to
> differences between the East and the West, to the significance of the
> dialectical theology in which he was profoundly interested. I voiced
> my great hope that the near future might witness the appearance
> of a genuinely "indigenous" Far Eastern Christian theology, and that
> it might help to dissolve the vicious antagonism between Continental
> and American theology by its radical contrast to both. He fully
> shared this hope. He confessed it as one of the ultimate objectives
> of their work. "What theology do you teach your students?" I in-
> quired, expecting that the answer would point either to traditional
> Dutch dogmatics or to the newer teaching of Karl Barth. "We try
> to introduce our students exclusively to the theology of the Bible.

Only from solid grounding in the Bible and in the Bible alone can come the new Christian theology for these younger churches which shall be both genuinely indigenous and truly Christian." He had laid his finger on the only possible seedplot not only for a sound indigenous theology but also for an adequate ecumenical theology for a united Christendom.[24]

These are queries, it will be agreed, which strike at the heart of the unfailing assumptions of our Western theology and theological instruction.

What effect would the outworking of an Asian or African Christian theology have upon the mind of the world church? At the least, one of correction and enrichment. From my own observations of the younger churches of the East and from reflection upon theological discussions at ecumenical conferences including Madras, I wrote in 1938:

> It is a commonplace that theological discussion among Christians of the West tends almost invariably to resolve itself into a debate between the Continental and American viewpoints with the British, in the position they delight to hold in theology no less than in politics, wielding the balance of power and mediating between their neighbors on either side. The understanding of Christian faith by Oriental Christians, however, if it has not been dominated by foreign teaching but springs spontaneously from direct and immediate apprehension, does not fall naturally upon the line along which almost the whole of Western theological discussion proceeds but upon quite other lines tangential to it. Their reflections move on an entirely new plane and in terms of quite other presuppositions than those which are axiomatic for Christians reared in the Western tradition. Many of the issues which preoccupy, and divide, traditional Christian theology seem to the Eastern thinker not so much unreal as secondary or even irrelevant. The accepted categories of debate do not commend themselves to him as valid or at any rate as vital. If it is insisted that discussion must be oriented to the prevailing Western perspective and carried forward in its habitual phrases, there can be no real meeting of minds.
>
> The first effect of this recognition is greatly to increase the complexities of discussion by shattering the accepted framework of traditional Western theology. The sharp antagonism between Continental and American contentions is dissolved, not by judicious compromise but by the introduction of a third or fourth point of reference of equal validity but quite different character. It suggests that the solution of the familiar antitheses of theological debate is not to be

24 Henry P. Van Dusen, *For the Healing of the Nations*, p. 53.

effected in an either/or choice or in facile reconciliation, but rather
in recognition that neither of the prevailing viewpoints or some
combination of them embraces the whole truth sought. The ultimate
result is immeasurably to enlarge and enrich one's realization of the
scope and range, the height and depth and breadth of Christian truth.

On the basis of these observations, I was led to a radical conclusion which almost a quarter century of continuous participation in ecumenical theological study and discussion have served
greatly to strengthen and to confirm:

> The ready and full expression of Christian faith in terms native
> and natural to Oriental minds has hardly begun. Some years will be
> required until a natural deference before the longer experience and
> readier confidence of historic Christianity can be overcome and the
> younger churches can bring their full contribution to the interpreta-
> tion of Christian faith. This participation must be encouraged and
> awaited for the future. When it comes, and only then, will the church
> of Christ in the world achieve its first truly ecumenical creed.[25]

At the least, such enrichment and correction should be the
outcome of the articulation of an "indigenous theology." But, at
the most, the development of Oriental and African Christian
theology *might* furnish an understanding and an interpretation
of Christian faith in the twentieth century that would require the
radical recasting of a Christian theology dominant in the Western
churches for nearly twenty centuries and heretofore unchal-
lenged. Nothing less than that is at stake in an indigenous theology of the younger churches!

Church Union

We have already noted more than once the central place that
organic Church Union holds—indeed, has held from earliest days
—in the total concern for *Christian unity* among the younger
churches.

The conception of the "ideal unity of the Church of Christ" is
by no means uniform or fixed in the views of Christians of the
older churches; and to this as yet unresolved, indeed as yet almost
unexamined, divergence in ideal, we shall need to return in Part
III as we cast our thought into the future.[26] Younger churchmen,
however, appear to hold a virtually single and unanimous conception of what the visible church of Christ, the existential

25 *Ibid.*, pp. 182–184.
26 See Part III, pp. 124 ff.

church, should be. They are able to rest content with nothing less than *one organically unified ecclesiastical structure,* a "corporeal unity" expressive of the "spiritual unity" of the body of Christ. This conviction was voiced in the moving plea of the leaders of the younger churches at the Madras Conference of 1938:

> The representatives of the younger churches, one and all, gave expression to the passionate longing that exists in all countries for visible union of the churches. . . . Visible and organic union must be our goal. . . . Such a union alone will remove the evils arising out of our divisions . . . the union for which our Lord prayed, through which the world would indeed believe in the Divine Mission of the Son, our Lord Jesus Christ.

The conviction was reiterated in "A Statement by Younger Church Delegates" at the Willingen Conference of the International Missionary Council in 1952:

> We believe that unity of the churches is an essential condition of effective witness and advance. In the lands of the younger churches divided witness is a crippling handicap. We of the younger churches feel this very keenly. While unity may be desirable in the lands of the older churches, it is *imperative* in those of the younger churches.[27]

I may be permitted the parenthetical judgment that, if this view of the ideal unity of Christ's church ultimately prevails throughout the world church, it will be less on grounds of either Biblical authorization or theological vindication than because the actual demonstration of such unity by the younger churches themselves has established its validity and its spiritual fruitfulness for all with eyes to see.

We have also taken note of the remarkable record of the younger churches in achieving organic church union. We reminded ourselves that the two most notable instances of church union in Christian history are achievements of younger churches, those in South India and in Japan; and that the two most noteworthy current proposals for further church union that are presently at a hopeful stage of discussion and negotiation likewise involve younger churches—those in North India and Ceylon. The three instances in India and Ceylon—one a realized union that has already celebrated a decade of tested experience, and the other two even now in the hands of the negotiating churches for decision—warrant special consideration.

[27] *The Missionary Obligation of the Church,* Willingen, 1952, p. 40 (italics in original).

The story of the Church of South India—the history of its long and often disheartening trials of exploration and discussion, its principles and plan of union, its coming into being in September, 1947, and even something of its remarkable achievements during these past thirteen years—is by now widely and well known.

It sought to unite representative churches drawn from the three major types of Protestantism—Anglican and Methodist, Presbyterian-Reformed, and Congregational. It took for its guiding principle the justly famous dictum of the Lausanne Conference on Faith and Order of 1927, twice repeated verbatim by the Second World Conference on Faith and Order at Edinburgh in 1937:

> In view of (1) the place which the Episcopate, the Councils of Presbyters, and the Congregation of the faithful, respectively had in the constitution of the early Church, and (2) the fact that episcopal, presbyteral, and congregational systems of government are each today, and have been for centuries, accepted by great communions in Christendom, and (3) the fact that episcopal, presbyteral, and congregational systems are each believed by many to be essential to the good order of the Church, we therefore recognize that these several elements must all, under conditions which require further study, have an appropriate place in the order of life of a reunited Church, and that each separate communion, recalling the abundant blessing of God vouchsafed to its ministry in the past, should gladly bring to the common life of the united Church its own spiritual treasures.[28]

Indeed, those who conceived the Church of South India carried these guiding principles one further step:

> It is sought to combine in the union three elements—the Episcopal, the Presbyterian, and the Congregational; and it is believed that each of these elements has been embodied. Comprehension and not limitation has been the aim. All that has been found helpful in the uniting Churches has been included, and each Church will find its special contribution enriched by what the others contribute.
>
> The Church of South India recognizes that episcopal, presbyteral, and congregational elements must all have their place in its order of life, and that the episcopate, the presbyterate, and the congregation of the faithful should all in their several spheres have responsibility and exercise authority in the life and work of the church, *in its governance and administration, in its evangelistic and pastoral work, in its discipline, and in its worship.*[29]

[28] *The Second World Conference on Faith and Order,* Edinburgh, 1937, p. 248.

[29] *Proposed Scheme of Church Union in South India,* pp. vii-viii, 7-8 (italics added).

As with every comprehensive scheme of church union, the uniting churches discovered the most formidable stumbling block to be the conception of the nature and authority of the ministry held by the several communions that proposed to unite. They "acknowledged each other's ministries to be real ministries of the Word and sacraments, and thankfully recognized the spiritual efficacy of sacraments and other ministrations which God has so clearly blessed."[30] They provided for episcopacy through the consecration of bishops by those who had themselves been consecrated by bishops holding authority in what is claimed to be an unbroken line from the first apostles. But they also provided that, during an exploratory period of thirty years, no specific steps should be taken to unify their several ministries by a formal act, in the confidence that since, during that period, all ministers would be episcopally ordained, at its close the Church of South India would in fact have achieved a unified ministry. To some of those who were most appreciative of the lofty hopes and goals of the Church of South India, this seemed a defect in the Plan of Union; and it is, indeed, precisely here that the most serious criticisms of the basis of the Church of South India have centered. This was the major ground of objection within the Anglican Communion to the recognition of the Church of South India as a true "sister church."

Those who have been seeking to evolve a true and sound plan of church union for North India and Ceylon have built directly on the South India labors, and gratefully acknowledge their indebtedness to the pioneers in South India. They, likewise, make their start from the Lausanne-Edinburgh formula, recognizing the three alternative conceptions of church order and ministries among the uniting communions—the episcopal, the presbyteral, and the congregational—and, as in South India, they propose to incorporate all three within a more comprehensive church order. But the plans in North India and in Ceylon differ from that of South India in two important respects.[31]

1. They are more comprehensive in that they hope to include not only the communions that united in South India—Anglican,

---

[30] *Ibid.*, p. 2.

[31] Although there are minor differences between the proposals for North India and those for Ceylon to which their respective representatives would doubtless wish to direct attention, none of these bears directly on the crucial issues; for most purposes, the two Plans may be regarded as alternative formulations of the same Scheme.

Congregational, Methodist, and Presbyterian-Reformed—but also Baptists. In the case of Ceylon, this means the complete roll of constituent churches of the National Christian Council. Because of the inclusion of Baptists, the provisions of the Plan with respect to the sacrament of Baptism are of paramount interest and importance. The essence of these provisions is that baptism of infants ("sponsored baptism") and baptism of adults on profession of faith ("believer's baptism") are recognized equally, and full membership in the church is to be through subsequent confirmation.

> A person may receive either sponsored baptism in infancy or believer's baptism. Where parents do not wish their children to receive sponsored baptism they shall bring them to a service of dedication.
> A person who has received sponsored baptism in infancy shall be admitted to communicant membership of the Church in a Service of Confirmation, such Service to provide for a candidate to accept and ratify the vows made on his behalf when he was baptized.[32]

The North India provisions with respect to baptism are similar.

2. Both Ceylon and North India propose to effect an immediate and full unification of the respective ministries of the uniting churches.

> The uniting Churches recognize that episcopal, presbyteral, and congregational elements all have their place in the order of life of the Church of Lanka, and that the episcopate, the presbyterate, the diaconate, and the congregation of the faithful should all, in accordance with their several functions, have responsibility and exercise authority in the life and work of the Church, in its governance and administration, in its evangelistic and pastoral work, in its discipline and in its worship.
> With respect to the initial ministry of the Church of Lanka, the uniting Churches desire the unification of the ministries of the several uniting Churches at the inauguration of union.

The "purpose and intention" of the uniting churches is to be set forth in a preface to be read at all rites to effect the desired unification:

> The good hand of God being upon us, these several Churches, called together into visible unity as a part of the Universal Church with an agreed basis of Faith and Order, desire, at the inauguration

[32] *Proposed Scheme of Church Union in Ceylon* (Third Revised Edition, 1955), pp. 13 f.

of union, by the use of the liturgical forms herein set forth, to bring about by God's grace and mercy such a unification of the sacred ministry in this Church as shall join together in one all the several inheritances of grace and authority which have hitherto been the possession of each Church in separation. In so doing, it is the intention of this Church to continue and reverently to use and esteem the threefold ministry of Bishop, Presbyter, and Deacon which existed in the undivided Church.

First, with respect to bishops:

The uniting Churches accept the historic episcopate, in a constitutional form, as part of their basis of union. By "historic episcopate" is meant the episcopate which has historic continuity with that of the undivided Church. No one particular theological interpretation of episcopacy shall be demanded from any minister or member of the Church of Lanka.

At the inauguration of union all those duly elected to be Bishops of the Church of Lanka who have not already received episcopal consecration shall be consecrated by three duly authorized Bishops, if possible from outside Ceylon, representing differing Church traditions and acceptable to all the uniting Churches. Immediately thereafter, all those who have been elected to be Bishops of the Church of Lanka and have been duly consecrated shall receive, by prayer and the laying on of hands by ministers of all the uniting Churches duly appointed for this purpose, a commission to exercise their ministry in the Church of Lanka.

The specific formula to be used in this service will be:

Forasmuch as you have been consecrated to the office and order of Bishop in the Church of God and have been elected to be Bishop in the Church of Lanka, we, on behalf of the uniting Churches, commission you as a Bishop of the Church of Lanka and acknowledge you to be now possessed of the fullness of the ministry of this Church in which are joined together our diverse ministries. The grace of the Holy Spirit be with you, enlightening, strengthening, and endowing you with wisdom all the days of your life, in the Name of the Father and of the Son and of the Holy Spirit. Amen.

The unification of ministries is to be effected in this fashion:

After the Bishops of the Church of Lanka have been elected, consecrated, and commissioned, each Bishop shall, with prayer and the laying on of hands, receive into the Presbyterate of the Church of Lanka all the ministers of the uniting Churches in his Diocese who desire to be Presbyters in the Church of Lanka, and are eligible to be so by their standing in their own Church.

The formula to be used at the laying on of hands will be:

> Forasmuch as you were called and ordained minister/priest/presbyter in the Church of God within the————Church, and are now called to a wider ministry in the Church of God as Presbyter within this Church of Lanka; receive from God the power and grace of the Holy Spirit to exercise this office in the Church of Lanka, and to nourish by Word and Sacraments all the members of Christ's flock within this Church of Lanka, in the Name of the Father and of the Son and of the Holy Spirit. Amen.
>
> Take authority to preach and teach the Word, to fulfill the ministry of reconciliation and to minister Christ's Sacraments in the congregation whereunto you shall be duly appointed. Amen.

On the much-mooted question of how this service is to be designated—whether "ordination" or "reordination" or "supplemental ordination" or "extension of orders" or "commissioning" or whatever—the authors of the Scheme have been led to this inspired formulation which both avoids the point of dispute and precisely reflects the spiritual realities:

> It is recognized that no name or title can be given to describe the nature of this service, as it has no historical precedent. The service is intended to be the means by which a new development in the restoration of the unity of the Church is effected.[33]

Such a method of achieving a mutually acceptable ministry was proposed as far back as 1920 by the Lambeth Conference of Anglican bishops in that year in their "Appeal to All Christian People":

> If the authorities of other Communions should so desire, we are persuaded that, terms of union having been otherwise satisfactorily adjusted, Bishops and clergy of our Communion would willingly accept from these authorities a form of commission or recognition which would commend our ministry to their congregations as having its place in the one family life.[34]

It will be recalled that the one blemish upon the achievement of the Church of South India—a very bitter disappointment to the leaders of that church and to Christians generally with a deep desire for church union—is the fact that the Church of South India did not succeed in preserving relations of full communion with churches of the Anglican fellowship, as had been hoped. The planners in Ceylon and North India have been at special

33 *Ibid.*, pp. 19 ff.
34 Quoted in Rouse and Neill, *op. cit.*, p. 447.

pains to seek to overcome the misgivings within Anglicanism
that might negate their great hope that the Church of Lanka
(Ceylon) might continue in relations of full communion with
the sister churches of the several uniting churches throughout
the world.

To anticipate these questions in advance of union, the proposals in Ceylon were considered at Lambeth in 1948. The Lambeth Conference declared:

> The Conference has learned with deep interest of the proposed
> scheme for Church Union in Ceylon, regards it as being, in many
> respects, among the most promising of the various schemes of its
> type in different parts of the world, and expresses the hope that . . .
> the projected union may, under the blessing of God, in due course
> be carried into effect.

And the Lambeth 1948 Committee on the Unity of the Church
hailed "the Ceylon Scheme as of singular interest and promise."[35]

A special and very weighty as well as representative Committee
of Anglican Theologians was appointed by the Archbishop of
Canterbury to advise him in this matter, with the late Bishop of
Derby (Dr. A. E. J. Rawlinson) as its chairman.

On the central question of the unification of ministries, this
committee reaffirmed the favorable word of Lambeth:

> Its members concurred with the judgment of the Lambeth Confer-
> ence to the effect that in general the Form proposed "would appear
> to satisfy the requirements for making the orders of the unified
> Ministry acceptable as valid without offence to the consciences of
> Anglicans."
> We believe that the wording of the rite expresses a sufficiently clear
> intention on behalf of the Church to secure for itself, through the
> action of God's Holy Spirit, such a fully unified Ministry: and in our
> judgment Presbyters thus commissioned should be accepted by the
> Anglican Churches as duly commissioned and authorized for the same
> office in the Church of God as are their own priests.

Both the Ceylon "Scheme" and the North India "Plan" were
subjected to thorough and critical re-examination by the Lambeth Conference of 1958, first in an extended report of the Committee on Church Unity and the Church Universal and then in
the full conference. With respect to the Ceylon proposal, note
was taken of certain changes in the Third Revised Edition of
1955 that satisfied misgivings which had been voiced by Lam-

[35] *Lambeth Conference, 1948* (S.P.C.K., London, 1948), pp. 41 f.

beth in 1948. One quite minor suggestion for further change
was offered. The committee's report was received and approved
by the conference itself: "The Conference endorses generally the
paragraphs of the Committee on Church Unity and the Church
Universal . . . and gives thanks to God for manifest signs of the
work of the Holy Spirit in the negotiations which have brought
the Scheme and Plan to this stage." Then, calling attention to the
single recommendation for further change, it declared: "The
Conference advises the Churches and Provinces of the Anglican
Communion that they should be willing to enter into full communion with the resulting Church of Lanka on its inauguration."[36]

If the proposed Church of Lanka comes into being, it will
represent the most comprehensive realization of church union in
Christian history. As a result, every principal Protestant Church
would be, directly or indirectly, in relationships of mutual recognition including intercommunion or of organic union with every
other.

IV

Making our start, as we do of preference, with broad matters of
achievement in co-operation, federation, and even church union,
we find our attention drawn toward the end to far more specific
issues of a theological nature—more particularly to the central
stumbling block for all efforts to effect the unity of the church of
Christ—the views regarding the origin, nature, and authority of
their respective ministries held by the several branches of Christendom; and the circumstances in which they can conceive of
themselves as entering into or maintaining relations of full recognition and fellowship, especially fellowship at the Table of the
Lord, with Christians of other names and heritages.

To this issue, we shall need to revert again, as we turn our
thoughts away from the past and the present, and attempt to
prospect the possibilities for a continuing, and possibly an accelerating, advance in *Christian unity* in the days immediately
ahead.

36 *The Lambeth Conference, 1958* (The Seabury Press, 1958), pp. 1, 36.

PART III

Tomorrow:

The Prospects for Christian Unity

We have surveyed the past. We have scrutinized the present. The time has come to direct our thought toward the future. What, if anything, can we say with some confidence about the world Christian movement tomorrow?

Let me make clear at the outset that we shall not attempt forecast or prophesy but, rather, an identification of some of the arresting prospects and some of the clamant problems that confront ecumenical Christianity as it advances into the second half of the twentieth century.

I

Let us begin with the more hopeful side of the picture—possibilities for the world Christian movement in the coming period.

The achievements of "The Great Century" suggest potentialities of Christian advance in the last half of the twentieth century surpassing those which have been realistic possibilities for any earlier epoch. We have repeatedly stressed the dual, or bifocal, character of this movement—*Christian missions* and *Christian unity*. If we imagine these two parallel and interrelated developments pressing forward along the same lines and at the same steadily accelerating pace through the next forty years, the dawn of the second Christian millennium might witness an approximation of the twofold goal of the acknowledgment of Christ throughout the earth and of the unity of a majority of his followers in one "great church."

i

To be sure, the ideal of all mankind brought into knowledge of Christ has commanded the leaders of the church from the earliest days and has furnished the theme not only for poets' dreams but also for prophets' forecasts. But those forecasts have usually been in the fevered accents of apocalyptic expectation and premised upon catastrophic supernatural intervention. Indeed, the incentive to reach every creature with the message of the gospel has often sprung from the conviction that this is the divinely appointed precondition for Christ's return in glory for judgment.

Seventy-five years ago, the company of ardent Christian youth who launched the Student Volunteer Movement for Foreign Missions boldly proclaimed as their watchword: "The Evangelization of the World in This Generation." We now know that this objective was inspired more by youthful daring than by a mature appraisal of the task. But today, with the instruments of mass communication already available, plus others which the coming years will almost certainly perfect, the attainment of the age-old Christian goal that every inhabitant of the earth shall have heard the message of Christ looms, for the first time, as a realistic possibility. This would not mean that every human being would profess allegiance to Christ, but that the proclamation of the gospel to every person would have been achieved.[1]

ii

Again, if we attempt to measure the outcome of another half century's progressive advance toward Christian unity, we are not justified in picturing that outcome in terms of a single church. To entertain such a hope is to fly in the face of the deeply rooted intransigence of the Roman Communion, and of the rapidly multiplying "sect" groups that presently hold aloof from ecumenical association. But that virtually all the rest of Christendom might by the year 2000 be embraced within a single community of mutual acknowledgment and mutually sustaining fellowship is not, granted an unbroken continuance of recent progress, beyond the limits of possibilities.

II

The record of "The Great Century" suggests such possibilities of Christian fulfillment by 2000. It does not guarantee them. On the contrary, only the irresponsible dreamer will deliberately blind his eyes to ominous countervailing factors which not only

---

[1] Contrary to a widely held misunderstanding, "evangelization" is not identical with "conversion." It refers to the *proclamation* of the Christian message rather than its *acceptance*.

threaten the hope of continuing advance but even imperil the amazing gains already won. It is essential to assess these negative prospects at their full weight.

i

No one should underestimate the sweep of recent Christian outreach. Nevertheless, it must be recognized that it has yet barely touched the fringes of that vast mass of humanity whom we still tend to speak of as the "non-Christian world." It is true that about one third of the earth's populace today professes at least formal Christian adherence. But outside Europe and America, Christians are as yet a numerically insignificant minority. In the continents of Asia, Africa, and Oceania, the proportion is scarcely more than 5 per cent.[2] Among the larger and more mature nations of the Orient, those brought into the church's membership seldom exceed 3 per cent. The great bulk of these people still acknowledge allegiance to one or another of the non-Christian faiths. Moreover, some of the latter are manifesting signs of revitalization, often reinforced by linkage with renascent nationalism. Islam, in particular, is today probably a more successful evangelizer than Christianity.

More ominous for the continued advance of the church is the unchecked spread of the Christian faith's two most powerful rivals for the allegiance of contemporary men—self-satisfied secularism and self-confident communism.

Even more far-reaching and more problematical in their final outcome are the revolutionary changes sweeping the two great continents where the world Christian mission had recorded its most notable advances and achieved its greatest strength, Asia and Africa.

Consider Africa. As recently as five years ago, Africa stood forth as the area of most promising Christian growth for the immediate future. Here Christian missions had claimed the adherence of the largest proportion of the populations—over 15 per cent. Nowhere else did Christian education exert such a predominant leadership. In the vast heart of the continent between the Sahara on the north and the Transvaal to the south, between 80 and 85 per cent of all primary and secondary schooling was in church and

[2] Compare *World Christian Handbook, 1957* (World Dominion Press, London, 1957), especially the summary statistical tables on p. 170. The editors of the handbook repeatedly warn that these figures are only approximate.

mission institutions. Even where the new national governments
were beginning to assume responsibility for the education of their
peoples, they were building upon solid Christian foundations
and were largely dependent upon Christian leaders. In the first
year of independence in Ghana, Prime Minister Nkrumah in-
stituted universal primary education almost overnight. I asked
the British Director of Education, who had stepped down to a
secondary position to make way for the new Ghanaian Minister of
Education, where they were discovering teachers to man the
two thousand new schools. He smiled and replied: "Oh, from the
mission schools, of course. There is no other source." Mr. Nkrumah himself testified that every single leader of the new nation
had had his preparation in Christian educational institutions.

Then came the catastrophic developments of 1960, in the
Congo and beyond. No one can possibly foresee whither these
revolutionary changes will lead. No one can forecast what will be
their ultimate effect upon the Christian churches and their allied
agencies. But the prospects are ominous.

A comprehensive survey of Christian missions at New Year
1949 carried the caption "Holding the Bridgeheads." The title
was well chosen. This does not imply that there are no new and
promising advances being pushed forward here and there, at
many different points, in various parts of the world. But the over-
all picture of the Christian world mission at the beginning of
the second half of the twentieth century is less that of triumphant
advance than that of a resolute holding operation. So far as one
can foresee the future, that promises to be its predominant character in the days ahead. It is no part of Christian optimism to
evade this threatening outlook, as it is no part of Christian real-
ism to permit it to chill the temper of Christian confidence or
cut the nerve of Christian effort.

The situation in areas traditionally Christian needs no exposition. Commenting upon the fact that the 1949 religious census
in the Uinted States revealed that somewhat over half of the
population are church members and that their number is still
increasing more rapidly than that of the total populace, Dr.
Samuel McCrea Cavert thus summarized a situation that is certainly not more unfavorable than in most nominally Christian
lands:

> There has never been a time in American history when so large
> a percentage of the people belong to the churches. . . . [But] those

who attend public worship regularly or in other ways participate actively in the life of the church are far fewer than those who call themselves members. . . . Any thoughtful observer would detect a disturbing discrepancy between the size of the churches and their influence on American life.

Christians are reluctant to admit that the strength and power for the advance of the church is, in appreciable measure, dependent upon political or economic factors in the general life of the times. But history shows conclusively that it is so. One of Dr. Latourette's most valuable services to our understanding of the logic of the expansion of Christianity is his clear delineation of successive epochs of advance and retreat, and his further conclusion that both progress and recession run parallel to, and are vitally influenced by, corresponding surges and setbacks in the fortunes of the cultures and states with which the church has become largely identified.[3] Moreover, he is certainly correct in linking "The Great Century" of Christian advance with the period of dominant ascendancy of Western civilization and, more particularly, in identifying the year 1914—the beginning of the epoch of the Great Wars—as the terminal date of that period. This does not necessarily imply that we have already entered upon another phase of recession, though there is sufficient evidence to prompt such a somber judgment. If subsequent events should confirm it, the First Assembly of the World Council of Churches at Amsterdam in 1948 would appear in the perspective of history as marking both the culmination of a century and a half of mighty achievement *and* the terminus of that unparalleled epoch. In any event, the responsible leadership of the Christian cause should be dismissed as blind leaders of the blind unless they are prepared to contemplate such a possibility, and to scan the future and lay their plans for it with such a possibility clearly in view.

ii

When we turn to the prospects for continuing progress in Christian unity, we may gladly recognize at once that the tidal currents which moved centrifugally within Christendom for eighteen centuries and then turned so mysteriously and marvel-

[3] Compare *The Unquenchable Light* and *Anno Domini, passim* (Harper & Brothers, 1941). Compare *World Christianity: Yesterday, Today, and Tomorrow*, pp. 57 ff.

ously toward the beginning of the nineteenth century are today
continuing to flow centripetally with steadily increasing power
and effect. The outlook for progressive fulfillment of Christ's
prayer that his followers should all be one is more promising than
it has ever been before.

Here, likewise, however, there are qualifying factors of which
full account must be taken.

We stand near the end, or perchance just past the end, of an
era whose underlying tendencies in the life of mankind were
centripetal, when the ends of the earth were becoming conscious
of one another and when that consciousness was parenting all
manner of world associations—scientific, cultural, educational,
political, economic, religious. The attempt, twice repeated in
thirty years, to achieve effective world political organization,
through the League of Nations and then the United Nations, is
at once the most ambitious and the most significant illustration.
The centripetal currents in the life of the churches at their inception flowed parallel to, if they were not wholly the spiritual expression of, wider centripetal tides in modern culture.

It is a principal glory of the ecumenical movement that, although it thus began when trends in general culture were almost
uniformly centripetal, it has continued with accelerating strength
after the general cultural drift had suffered radical reversal under
the pressures of mighty centrifugal forces which today appear to
dominate the world of nations.

Nevertheless, a world rifted by division and conflict is an un-
propitious setting for any effort toward Christian unity on a
global scale. Contemporary political tensions have not only
spurred Christians to present a more united witness. They have
also lifted barriers between Christians of the largest and most
influential Orthodox communion, that of Russia, and Christians
in China and North Korea on the one hand, and the rest of Christendom. Thus far, heroic determination to preserve ecumenical
fellowship has prevented the rising of similar barriers between
other Christians on opposite sides of the several "curtains," in
Central Europe and in Asia. But long continuance of the conflict
of East and West, and its steady exacerbation, would certainly
render that fellowship increasingly difficult.

Again, it is well to recall that trends of thought tend to move
by a logic of oscillation from one direction to another, often from
one extreme to its opposite. One generation or epoch discerns

the onesidedness of its predecessor, "discovers" essential truth overlooked by those persons who have gone before, magnifies the neglected truth as though it were truth itself, and thus gives its whole allegiance to a portion of genuine truth with an exaggeration sometimes as onesided as that from which it is in reaction. The succeeding generation or epoch is likely to repeat the process in the reverse direction.

The bearing of this inherent dialectic upon our concern is obvious. Christians and their churches are all too susceptible to the same logic of oscillation. We may anticipate that ecumenical developments will be subject to challenge from powerful counter tendencies. Question will be pressed whether this movement of Christian unity, this ecumenical Christianity, is not sweeping too rapidly and perhaps has already gone too far. It will be suggested that unity is purchased at the sacrifice of essential principles, that it can be grounded only on the insecure foundation of a least common denominator. Some such charge is already being whispered where it is not openly declared.

It should be admitted that there is always some truth in such reaction. As just suggested, powerful trends do neglect aspects of familiar and established truth in their enthusiasm for other and previously denied aspects of truth newly discovered. When such an inevitable dialectical swing is supported by dominant currents in the life and thought of the times, it may portend opposition to the movement for Christian unity which it has not had to face in the epoch of its recent great advance.

All this lends additional reason and urgency for a thoroughly realistic examination and appraisal of the major issues confronting Christian unity in the days immediately ahead.

III

No one who attempts to survey the total reality of the Christian world movement today in comprehensive and dispassionate perspective can escape the conviction that ecumenical Christianity is approaching, if it does not already stand within, a time of crisis, of fundamental and far-reaching transition.

This statement is much more than a reiteration of the familiar platitude: *"Now* is an hour of crisis." *This* is a crisis in the special sense of a necessary, inescapable transition, a transition dictated by the inherent logic of development. This is true at every level: on the world scene, within most nations, and in local communities.

Moreover, it is a crisis pregnant with two alternative and antipodal possibilities. It is a law of life, institutional no less than individual, that we must go forward or we shall certainly go backward.[4] More than that, as in the careers of persons, so institutions and movements come to decisive forks in the road that *must* be taken—to right or left, to right or wrong; and the turning at those crucial forks determines the direction and development for the whole course beyond. There is reason to think that ecumenical Christianity confronts such a determinative fork or complex of forks.

On the *world scene,* the World Council of Churches was brought to formal birth in an atmosphere of quite extraordinary good will and under an aura of extravagant expectation.

Furthermore, if one may continue the metaphor, the World Council came officially to birth after a period of unique gestation, gestation, so to say, not in the dark womb of discussion and planning but in intense and testing activity under the brilliant spotlight of a world at war. In the perspective of history, it may be seen that the forced delay of almost a decade in the formal constituting of the World Council may have been a providential provision for its health. The "ten formative years" (1938–1948) offered its responsible leaders an opportunity—rather, imposed upon them the necessity—to give the new body virtually complete structure in skeleton and a fully developed program without official authorization. A distinguished leader of American Lutheranism returned from his first visit to World Council headquarters at Geneva in the winter of 1946 with this comment: "They say the World Council of Churches is yet to be born. It must be the liveliest embryo this planet has ever seen."

As a result, the World Council came formally into being not as a puling infant but as a vigorous adolescent, having experienced many of the growing pains of childhood and the crises of youth. It is a tribute to the perception, foresight, and wisdom of

4 This point is more fully developed on pp. 132 ff.

those charged with its care during the war and the immediate postwar decade that when the officially appointed obstetricians and wet nurses assembled at Amsterdam to bring it formally to birth, they could find so little in the youth that required amputation or alteration. The World Council of Churches of the "ten formative years" became the World Council of Churches of the "first six years."

The World Council has passed successfully through the initial stages of its life—birth and infancy and youth. It has domesticated itself within the consciousness of the leadership of the member churches. However, there are signs that, in some quarters at least, the first flush of enthusiasm has begun to wane. Certainly, its inherent limitations and stresses have emerged more clearly. And questions that heretofore had lain dormant or had been barely murmured are beginning to be pressed with firm insistence.

At the *national level,* certainly in the United States, a "time of testing" likewise appears imminent. The National Council of Churches has also experienced its birth throes. We all rejoice in its coming into existence. We marvel at the skill of *its* obstetricians and midwives. Does history—certainly church history—record a more careful, patient, persistent, and successful achievement of institutional reordering than the merging of twelve national interdenominational bodies into one, especially the winning of consent (and, in most instances, convinced and enthusiastic approval) by the several hundred official church bodies —denominations, boards, and agencies—whose affirmative vote was the precondition for the actual constituting of the National Council of Churches? We stand in awe—when we do not stand aghast—at the complexity and intricacy of the resulting organizational structure, "beyond challenge, the most complex and intricate piece of ecclesiastical machinery this planet has ever witnessed." But already its friendliest critics are raising questions; difficult issues of transition loom for early confrontation.

The National Council of Churches in the United States is *sui generis.* In other countries, the problems of transition are, on the surface at least, rather different; but the underlying issues are often akin. National Councils of Churches elsewhere—so often created after and in response to developments on the world scene, thus reversing the generally accepted logic of normal and healthy evolution—have scarcely yet established their *raison d'être*. Here, again, one fact is clear: they must go forward or they shall certainly slide backward.

At the *local level,* in cities and communities, it is an accepted axiom of Christian unity in our day that the most critical question for the whole ecumenical development in the period through which we are passing is: Will ecumenical Christianity, which thus far has developed for the most part *not* from the grass roots upward as democratic theory prescribes for healthy organisms *but* from the top downward, now achieve "grass rootage"?

Our major concern is with world ecumenicity, and with national and local ecumenicity only as they affect vitally the world movements. But we do well to bear in mind also the crisis at the lesser levels of nation and community, for there is intimate and reciprocal relationship among them all.

IV

What, then, are the major issues confronting ecumenical Christianity at this moment of transition? Let us consider four:

 i. Problems implicit in the transfer of leadership from the persons who so largely guided the destinies of the movement in the days of its projection and early development to those officially designated by the member churches for its direction.

 ii. The role of councils of churches—local, national, and world—within ecumenical Christianity.

 iii. The relation of *world interdenominationalism* and *world confessionalism,* i.e., of ecumenism and denominationalism.

 iv. The relations of *Christian missions* and *Christian unity,* especially of the International Missionary Council to the World Council of Churches.

i

Among the closest friends and well-wishers of both the World Council of Churches and the National Council of Churches

U.S.A., a spirited debate is now in progress. It focuses on the question whether the free and prophetic leadership that played the major role in both the initiation and the early development of these bodies can continue with undiminished influence now that the councils have come under the direction of the official representatives of their member churches. This is a pressing question for ecumenism at every level. And it is an issue for the Christian world mission as well as within the movement for Christian unity. Indeed, it is a matter on which the history of Christian missions in the modern period casts especially revealing light.

The logical mind would prefer to suppose that ecumenical Christianity in each of its two major branches—Christian missions and Christian unity—and at all levels is the direct creation of the churches acting through their officially designated and authorized leaders. Actually, anyone passingly familiar with the history of Christian missions knows well how far from the facts such a supposition moves. As we have observed, the initial impulses of the modern missionary movement arose *not* from within the regular structures of the existing churches and under the guidance of their accredited officers but for the most part *outside* those structures and under the leadership of men and women who, although devout Christians and loyal church members, were not participants in the ecclesiastical hierarchies. Witness the founding of the London Missionary Society, the American Boards for both Foreign and Home Missions and the Bible Societies, the influence of the "haystack" group at Williams, and countless other examples. Almost all the earliest, most daring, and most prophetic expressions of nineteenth-century missionary advance were, in the strict sense, nondenominational; only later were their vision and their achievements domesticated within the established church structures.

Very similar have been the origins and early phases of the movement for Christian unity. In large measure, they were the creation of devout Christians and loyal church members but persons without major status and responsibilty within their respective ecclesiastical bodies. Even such prominent exceptions as Archbishop Söderblom and Archbishop Temple, who might seem to disprove the generalization, would have insisted on their indebtedness to John R. Mott, J. H. Oldham, William Adams Brown, William Paton, W. A. Visser 't Hooft, etc., none of whom held ecclesiastical office. In the United States, it is almost an axiom that early ecumenical leadership came from outside rather than from within the ranks of official denominational leadership.

A single but not unrepresentative instance may serve as illustration. In preparation for the Oxford Conference of 1937 on Church, Community, and State, the international planning committee drew up a panel of persons whom it considered indispensable for the leadership of the conference. The list included thirty American Christians—the North American President and Secretary of the Universal Christian Council for Life and Work, which was the sponsoring body, the presiding officer of the conference, the chairmen of two of the five sections and the secretary of another, four or five platform speakers, a dozen theologians and laymen whose participation on drafting committees was felt to be of first importance. The total membership of the conference was fixed at four hundred, with three hundred places allocated to the official delegates of the churches; among these, eighty were assigned to American denominations. When the latter forwarded their lists of officially appointed delegates, of the thirty Americans whom the Planning Committee regarded as essential to the highest effectiveness of the conference, just one had been named as a regular delegate by his own church. For example, four places had been assigned to the Presbyterian Church U.S.A. But among the members of that church who were considered indispensable for the leadership of the Oxford Conference were Dr. William Adams Brown, as the American President of the Universal Christian Council; Presidents Henry Sloane Coffin and John A. Mackay, who had been selected as chairmen of two of the five sections; Prof. John C. Bennett, to serve as secretary of another section; Drs. Samuel McCrea Cavert and Henry P. Van Dusen, who were to give major addresses; Mr. John Foster Dulles, Dr. Roswell P. Barnes, etc. Not one of these Presbyterians was named by his church among its four delegates. Fortunately, one fourth of the total of four hundred places had been reserved for co-opted members; all but one of the Americans named by the Planning Committee as "indispensable" were appointed in that category. The principle of co-option is regarded with intense suspicion and distaste by many ecclesiastical officers. Nevertheless, this is the device by which the presence of many of the best equipped, most valuable, and most influential participants has been secured for the great majority of the major ecumenical gatherings.

The ecumenical movement, in both its American and its world organs, stands today at a moment of fateful transition marked by the transfer of responsibility for its direction from the hands of a relatively small group of men and women of pioneering vision, spirit, and conviction who brought it to birth ("ecumaniacs," they have been affectionately dubbed) into the hands of a very much larger number of denominational officials and spokesmen ("ecclesiastical wheelhorses," they have been called), many of them by temperament and habit cautious and conservative, who had a minor part in the creation of the movement, but who now (because of its basic character as the creature of its member churches) must guide its future. The transfer of responsibility is an accomplished fact and will not be reversed; there can be no return to the control of the "prophets." But the outcome of that transition for the life of the ecumenical organizations, whether continuing vitality and growth or stagnation or lingering death, is still to be determined. Which of these alternatives is to prevail depends on whether this transition can be effected without the by-product that has accompanied so many similar transitions in Christian history—the quiet and gradual but firm elimination of the most creative minds and courageous wills.

This issue was the subject of vigorous discussion at the annual meeting of the United States Conference for the World Council of Churches at Buck Hill Falls in April, 1960. The discussion was initiated by a provocative paper by the Rev. Walter D. Wagoner which laid down the premise:

> The W.C.C., through no fault of its own, is now subject to the same transitional tensions, dangers, and opportunities which confront any worthy movement after the days of its youth. It is becoming more institutionalized, more settled in its ways. And although the W.C.C. is not a church, it does face the same sociological and morphological pressures and patterns as do all new churchly movements.

Mr. Wagoner pointed to three tensions:

> *There is a tension between form and spirit:* . . .
> The inevitable result is that the spirit of the ecumenical movement as manifest in the W.C.C. is more and more expressed in certain regularized forms. The time always approaches when an army leaves its tents behind and builds a fortress . . . or when tabernacles are built on the Mountain of Transfiguration.
> *There is the tension between the new—the volunteer, the unorthodox, and the old—the professional, the orthodox.*

As the W.C.C. becomes more organized it is only natural and inevitable that paid staff increases (even if pay does not) and that
ecclesiastics and clergy run the organization. . . . One observes, for
example, that denominational delegations to the coming New Delhi
Assembly are, with good reason, obligated to give room within their
quotas to persons of long experience in the ecumenical movement,
to persons moreover who are built into the organization charts of the
W.C.C. This means perforce that there is less room for new faces,
new ideas, and future leadership training. . . .

*There is the tension between stereotyped and experimental ecumen-
ical strategies. . . .*

What must we make of the fact that the leadership of the W.C.C.
seems to be increasingly, ex officiis, the leadership of the member
churches? Do these facts in any way inhibit the degree to which the
W.C.C. may prophetically criticize both itself and its member
churches?

We have mentioned the method employed to assure the presence and participation of nonecclesiastical representatives of independent thought and vigorous initiative in ecumenical conferences, either as co-opted members or as consultants. In the regular
functioning of the ecumenical councils themselves, the same end
is secured by the practice of opening membership on commissions
and committees to persons who are not official delegates to the
council, although such appointments are normally subject to
scrutiny and approval by the church to which each appointee be-
longs. It is in such commissions and committees that the major
part of the basic and creative thinking and planning takes place.
The result is a logical anomaly: much of the most important
work of the council is being performed by those who are not the
officially appointed spokesmen of the member churches; the
function of the latter with respect to new developments in either
thought or program is largely confined to review and confirmation.

This situation is inescapably disclosed at the annual gathering
of the World Council of Churches committees. The complex of
meetings that extend over the better part of a month breaks into
two distinct parts.

First, twenty or thirty committees and subcommittees charged
with planning and supervising every aspect of the World Council's multifarious and ever-enlarging program assemble. The
participants in these groups may total two hundred to two hundred and fifty persons. The atmosphere is informal and relaxed.
Discussion is spirited, controversy is uninhibited, ideas and sug-

gestions range widely and freely. And from these deliberations emerge the concrete proposals for the work of the Council's divisions and departments for the period immediately ahead.

Then, most of the program planners depart and the policy-determining Central Committee of the World Council convenes. It is composed of ninety official representatives of the member churches, surrounded by one hundred to one hundred and fifty consultants, observers, visitors, staff, etc. The setting is necessarily official and formal. In so large a deliberative body, genuine discussion is limited and often ponderous, controversy is minimal, attention focuses for the most part upon a vast accumulation of administrative matters *and* upon a critical review of proposals coming from the many preliminary meetings that have just adjourned.

For example, at St. Andrews, Scotland, in August, 1960, the meeting of the Central Committee was preceded by no fewer than thirty-five divisional, departmental, and other preparatory committee meetings, plus a very important consultation on evangelism at Bossey in July, which is not included in the figures that follow. The role of those in attendance upon these gatherings (not including wives, husbands, children, and friends) was 432, of whom 89 were staff. Of the 343 participants other than staff, 250 came for the preliminary meetings of the first fortnight. The attendance at the Central Committee itself totaled 146. Thus, there was an overlap of 57 persons who were present throughout, of whom some 30 were Central Committee members and about as many were consultants, visitors, etc.

No one who has had the privilege over a number of years of sitting successively in these two types of World Council gatherings could fail to be impressed, and sometimes depressed, by the contrast. It can be recorded with confidence that the participants in the program-planning committees and subcommittees report each year an increasingly exciting and rewarding experience. It must be added that a number of the most faithful and valued members of the policy-determining Central Committee confess privately their deepening concern and apprehension over what they believe to be an increasing formalism, conservatism, and unreality in the Central Committee's procedures from year to year.

In the National Council of Churches in the U.S.A.—and doubtless in other countries also—this issue appears in somewhat different form. The very large membership of the American Council's

General Board makes possible more numerous and more diversi-
fied denominational representation; and the officers of several of
the member churches have been at pains to assure participation
by some of their younger and more forward-looking men and
women. On the other hand, the very size and complexity of the
National Council tend to aggravate the inherent tendency of all
ecclesiastical bodies toward ponderous procedures and cautious
decisions.

We have called attention to the logical anomaly in the present
situation. And we have suggested that church officials tend to dis-
like and distrust the device of co-option, or consultants, which is
the source of the anomaly. More than that; since they constitute
the core of the official membership of the church councils, they
are always in a position to negate the influence of bolder and
more progressive individuals functioning in a consultative capacity, or to tether or even silence them.[5]

We have posed the problem in the context of the immediate
fact of transfer of leadership and, for purposes of illustration,
mainly in terms of the present situation in two particular ecumenical bodies, the World Council and the American National
Council. But the issue involved is a much larger and more general one. It is the role of independent, progressive, and sometimes
radical individuals and groups within movements that are preponderantly ecclesiastical in structure and control. It is basically
the age-old tension between the prophetic and the priestly elements within the church of Christ. Can ecumenical Christianity
in its various expressions learn the manifest lesson of Christian
history and be bold enough to insist that this tension shall *not*
be resolved (almost always, in the past, through the dominance
of the ecclesiastical and the suppression or emasculation of the
prophetic) but, rather, that the testing and painful tension shall
be deliberately maintained by provision within the ecumenical
organizations for equal participation and equal influence by both
wings of the church?

When the issue is so seen, especially against the background of
"The Great Century," it is obvious that the stake of Christian
missions is no less than that of Christian unity.

[5] For a fuller and balanced consideration of the basic issue, see the discussion between Dr. John C. Bennett, Dr. Eugene Carson Blake, and the present
writer in *Christianity and Crisis* (January 7, May 12, and July 7, 1952).

ii

A second issue that also lies within the life of the ecumenical movement itself concerns the role of church councils—more particularly the place of local councils of churches in the structure of national councils of churches and the place of the latter in the World Council, i.e., the relation of *local ecumenicity to national ecumenicity* and of *national ecumenicity* to *world ecumenicity*.

There is a contradiction at the heart of the conciliar development itself that cries for correction.

It is an accepted dogma of popular democratic theory that any sound development should originate in local communities—at the grass roots—and then work upward and outward, to state and national and finally international levels.

On the other hand, it is a widely held axiom of ecumenical history that the modern advance in Christian unity in almost every aspect has originated at the world level and then worked inward and downward to the national and ultimately the local levels.

Neither generalization is altogether true.

Very few, if any, major democratic developments have originated at the grass roots, i.e., in local communities. Almost always, they have been born in the imagination and determination of a few, a very few, leaders who have won for them—often with blood and sweat and tears—the late and skeptical and reluctant support of the masses.

So, likewise, as we have pointed out above, ecumenical Christianity, especially in the United States, had its origin in the vision and dedication of a relatively few ecumenical enthusiasts. Only recently, very tardily, has it begun to come alive within local communities.

On the other hand, the ecumenical axiom—that Christian unity began first at the world level and only later took form at the national level and finally at the local level—is a half-truth, almost exactly one half of the truth.

The fact is that ecumenicity in virtually all its major forms —co-operation of individual Christians across denominational lines, nondenominational fellowships such as the Christian youth and student movements, nondenominational and interdenominational[6] conferences, interdenominational and interchurch councils, organic church unions—has developed first within one or more nations, then at the world level, and lastly—often at long last—locally.

The earliest agencies of nondenominational co-operation—missionary and Bible societies—were all *national* bodies, originally of individual Christians, animated by a world outlook and purpose. National student Christian movements prepared the way for the World Student Christian Federation. The Foreign Missions Conference of North America antedated the International Missionary Council by a quarter of a century. As we remarked in the preceding chapter, the earliest significant *interchurch* body in Christian history was the Federal Council of Churches of Christ in the United States (1908). To be sure, the Federal Council had been preceded by a few, perhaps twelve or fifteen, pioneering councils of individual Christians—and possibly of churches—in states and local communities. Doubtless these furnished precedents and encouragement to the prophetic spirits who conceived the Federal Council. Nevertheless, it was the creation of the Federal Council that led to the prodigious proliferation of state and local councils of churches, rather than the reverse. It is not yet fully appreciated how far the Federal Council prospected the pathway and pioneered the pattern for all types of interchurch collaboration that have been achieved in this century. Its example worked out across the world to inspire the World Council of Churches and, through it, church councils in a score of countries; it worked down into nearly a thousand states, counties, cities, and towns in the United States alone, not to speak of a steadily mounting number of similar bodies in other lands.

Nevertheless, with due recognition of the qualification with respect to the *initial* instances of varied types of co-operation, the axiom on the whole holds. It was the launching of the *International* Missionary Council in 1921 that led immediately and directly to the founding of *national* Christian councils in India, Japan, and China, and subsequently to national Christian councils in over forty other countries. It was the projection of the

6 "Nondenominational" denotes co-operation of individuals or groups belonging to different denominations, but not official church co-operation. "Interdenominational" or "interchurch" refers to official action of churches or of church bodies such as mission boards.

World Council of Churches in 1937 that prompted the creation of *national* councils of churches since that date in some twenty lands. Thus, although the first experiments in a few nations, principally India and North America, established precedents for corresponding *world* movements, it has been the world bodies which, by and large, have provided the incentives and the examples for the rapid spread of ecumenicity within other nations.

As for the chronological and causal relationship between *national* and *local* ecumenicity, again—with some notable exceptions—the same sequence has held. Most expressions of *local* ecumenicity have been inspired by the example of *national* ecumenicity.

Moreover, it is a truism of ecumenical history that, broadly speaking, the modern development of *Christian unity* in almost every aspect has gone forward faster and farther at the world level than at the national level, faster and farther at the national than at the local level. Today, *Christian unity* is most advanced and strongest where one would expect unity to be most difficult to achieve and maintain—on the world scene; least vital where it should be easiest and inevitable—in villages and towns and cities. What we have said of the reality of *Christian unity* is truer of the world church than of churches within nations; truer of national church bodies than of local congregations. It is probably not an exaggeration to say that the leaders of world ecumenicity know one another more intimately, trust one another more fully, and co-operate with one another more effectively than do church officers of different denominations within most nations; and that the latter know each other more intimately, trust each other more fully, and join mind and hand and act far more continuously and effectively than do the ministers of their several denominations within most local communities.

In many countries, national councils of churches, called into being after and often in direct response to the example of the World Council are still pitifully weakling bodies. Their rightful place and functions both within the church life of their respective countries and in relation to the several world ecumenical bodies have still to be discovered and defined. In part, this is the inevitable result of the basic principle of the organization of the World Council, that its membership consists of autonomous national churches. Inevitably, officers of these churches have recognized a more commanding duty to render ecumenical service on the world level than within their own nations. In some instances, we confront the anomaly of participation by a national church within the World Council without the acceptance by that church of any responsibility whatever to fulfill within its own country the obligations of Christian co-operation and unity in relation to its fellow member churches of the World Council from the same nation.

When we turn to ecumenical relationships within local communities, in most countries and communities the realization of local ecumenicity has hardly begun. One can cite from personal knowledge not two or three but scores of instances where the officials of national churches (i.e., denominations) work day in and day out in the closest and most demanding collaboration as though they were in truth co-officers of the universal church of Christ while the local representatives of those same denominations in countless cities and towns, whatever their personal associations as fellow citizens, have virtually no relationships with one another as Christians and churchmen. Here is perhaps the most flagrant, as it is certainly the most inexcusable, illustration of the "scandal of our divisions" in the contemporary life of Christ's church. As Dr. Visser 't Hooft has declared: "The most important witness of the Christian church is its local witness. . . . We must think very especially of its role in a given village or city, . . . of its privilege to demonstrate on the spot what true human solidarity means."[7] In this passage, Dr. Visser 't Hooft is writing of "the church as a watchman or guardian in society." How much truer is his statement if we are thinking of the church as a witness to Christ's universal church! This contradiction between genuine and effective ecumenicity at the world and national levels on the one hand and unmodified and often unrepented particularism and denominationalism at the grass roots goes far to make a mockery of our professions of Christian unity. If we cannot or will not make the effort to learn to know one another and to work actively and worship worthily as Christian brethren where people live and where the church of Christ has its foundational reality, much of the talk of ecumenicity in the stratospheric atmosphere of world gatherings and world bodies will strike outsiders as the veriest pretense, if not hypoc-

[7] W. A. Visser 't Hooft, *The Renewal of the Church* (The Westminster Press, 1957), p. 116.

risy. Dare we attempt to refute their disdain? More than that, how long can world or national ecumenicity endure without sound and secure rootage in local communities?

These things ought not to be. Unless the whole ecumenical development succeeds in effecting Christian unity in local communities in the very near future, it will become infected with a larger measure of unreality than now prevails. For the pretension of Christian unity on a world or national scale while Christians and churches in communities continue in unreconstructed division and distance is palpable even if unrecognized insincerity. It is the kind of pretense that sours alike the souls of men and institutions. Such unreality and insincerity may presage stagnation and ultimate futility for national and world ecumenicity. Actually, the contradiction of the present situation is infecting the whole ecumenical development to a larger degree than is generally recognized.

To put the same point positively: if Christian unity is to be real, it must come alive where people live—in towns and cities and hamlets. Any other kind of ecumenicity is abstract, theoretical, problematic. Sad to say, that is the inner character of much national and world ecumenicity today.

In summary, the first imperative for the period immediately ahead is the realization of Christian unity at the grass roots, in local communities. It is no less mandatory than the completion of the several supremely significant church unions, e.g., Ceylon, North India, etc., now hanging in the balance.

But if this imperative is to be heeded and obeyed, two major conversions must take place. There must be a conversion, e.g., an about-face, in the conviction of most of the foremost ecumenical leaders as to the importance and urgency of local ecumenicity, as to the crucial role of local councils of churches in the over-all fulfillment of Christian unity in our day. On the other hand, there must be a radical reconception and reconstruction, an about-face, in the philosophy, structure, functions, and programs of local ecumenicity as it exists today, certainly in the United States, if it is to be worthy of its rightful place.

Consider the place that local ecumenicity holds in the conviction and concern of responsible church leaders. What is the present role of most local church councils, not in their own thought but in the view of the two corporate realities to which they are related—the community and the churches? Figures that would suggest the latter's view of the community council of churches are:

1. *A messenger boy, a useful servant*—to do for them all sorts of rather secondary but necessary things that they are too busy to do themselves (special seasonal services, radio ministry, institutional chaplaincies, etc.).

2. *A circus master* who, on occasions of public demonstration (Reformation Day, World Day of Prayer services, etc.), marshals all the churches in spectacular and harmonious parade.

3. *A telephone exchange, a message center, and clearinghouse.*

4. *A symbol:* a symbol of united Christendom, the body of Christ. A symbol is a sign, not itself the reality, pointing toward the reality that it represents. In this instance, the pointing is forward in time, to the future. A council of churches suggests a reality that is yet to be: a united church of Christ.

But the main work of the church still goes on in individual denominational congregations. As Dr. Truman Douglass has commented with devastatingly acute perception: "The denominations . . . retain for themselves most of the exhilarating opportunities for Christian action. The tasks delegated to the councils tend to be either ecclesiastically unprofitable functions or the kind of errands that can only be classified as religious and ethical trivialities."[8]

What *should be* the role of the local church council in the community and among the churches?

Let us take one of these figures—the message center. That rightly suggests the centrality of the council with respect to geographical location, usually somewhere near the heart of the community. A message center may be thought of as a place where ideas and plans are received, organized, and transmitted. It does *not* originate that which it transmits.

Now, let us infuse that analogy with life by translating the inert figure of mechanism into a figure of ancient and sacred Christian standing, that of the body.

At once, the proper role of the church council becomes clear. It should be the heart—the heart of a body of which Christ is the head and the individual churches are the limbs. It should be the

8 Dr. Douglass is here referring to church councils in general, but his diagnosis applies particularly to local ecumenicity. See his paper "Our Cooperative Witness to Our Oneness in Christ," *The Christian Century* (January 8, 1958).

source of vitality from which energies flow out into members and through them on into the larger amorphous organism, the community.

What kind of vitality? Action? Activity? Yes, but not that only. Rather, each of the three familiar types of vitality that, according to an ancient and not-yet-outmoded understanding of human nature, together constitute the whole person: intellectual, spiritual, volitional. There are three types of leadership to be expected from local councils of churches.

1. *Leadership in Thought.* It should be the intellectual center of the churches in the community. Better thinking—keener, wiser, profounder—should go on in the offices of the church council than in the study of any pastor. Not only thinking concerning church strategy, though that, but also thinking concerning Christian ethical principles and Christian faith. And, since the distinctive kind of thinking that the churches are supposed to carry on is theological, the church council should be the locus of the ablest theological thinking in the community.

There are two groups among whom that leadership should be mainly exerted:

a. *Clergy:* through clergy retreats, theological discussion groups, etc.

b. *Laity:* both men and women. Note here the contemporary hunger of the more thoughtful laity for theological guidance and instruction—a hunger that no single church or denomination is able to satisfy.

The indirect and incidental result should be the best possible contribution to the development within the churches of an ecumenical theological mind—not a new theology, a least common denominator, but an ecumenical understanding and outlook, a recognition of the extent and richness of the already existing ecumenical consensus.

2. *Leadership in Worship*—in the nurture of the inner life of the spirit. Not simply days or services for united prayer, though that. (Too often these are, inevitably, somewhat theatrical, eclectic, eccentric.) But also the development of personal spiritual life at a level deeper as well as broader than any individual church or denomination can nurture; for example, through lay retreats for both men and women and clergy retreats under leadership of superlative competence, not so readily available to any particular congregation or denomination. The indirect and incidental re-

sult should be the gradual development among the churches in the community of an ecumenical spiritual unity.

3. *Leadership in Action.* Here much is already under way and has already been accomplished; mainly, however, action on the social front. What is here suggested is that the council of churches should become the leader, the heart, the source of vitality for dynamic spiritual activity. Such spiritual outreach must be principally in two directions:

a. *Across the world:* the missionary outreach of the churches. Today this is the proper logic of missionary education and advance. Church councils are more accurate opposite numbers to many of the united younger churches than are the denominations.

b. *In the community:* The harsh truth is: there is not one major problem of the community—political, social, spiritual—not one, upon which the churches can make a significant, an appreciable, impact by congregations or even by denominations. For example: *political corruption*—in many communities that, through most of the years of most of our lifetimes, have suffered under the benevolent misrule of corrupt and conscienceless party machines—political corruption that ever threatens to raise its head and bring our cities under its heel. Or: *prostitution, narcotics, alcoholism, juvenile delinquency*—endemic diseases within the body politic. Or: better *housing,* more adequate *education, social improvement* of every kind. Not one of these community evils crying for elimination can be effectively mitigated, not one of the advances crying for implementation can be significantly furthered by individual congregations or single denominations—not one.

And, when we bring our attention close home and face the churches' first and most clamant responsibility—the tens of thousands, hundreds of thousands, who are wholly outside any effective contact with Jesus Christ and his gospel, the churches' most flagrantly bypassed job, evangelism—the bald fact is the same: impotence in separation. Our sin is not merely the "scandal of our denominationalism," of which we so often and so glibly repent. It is, no less—the impotence of our parochialism. And that requires "amendment of life." No single congregation, no individual denomination, can possibly undertake or effectively carry through a program and effort of evangelism adequate to the unfinished task—the largely bypassed task—of reaching the unchurched and ex-churched thousands in any community. Here is the urgent, clamant inescapable ecumenical imperative for every city and town—ecumenical evangelism, united evangelism, not merely through interdenominational evangelistic meetings but, more important, through a unified strategy, pooling and deployment of resources so that the whole strength of the whole church of Christ in any community shall be focused unitedly upon unremitting endeavor to win its citizens and its corporate life into obedience to the one Head of the church, who is also the one rightful Lord of Life.

To each of these problems, to every one of the churches' most urgent tasks, there is only one answer: the massed Christian strength of all churches directed unitedly upon common responsibilities. Unity is, first of all, the clear counsel of expediency, of practical statesmanship. The indirect but inevitable result should be the ecumenical unity of the churches.

The most urgent imperatives for local councils of churches in the years immediately ahead spring in part out of their obligations and opportunities for service to national and world ecumenism, in part out of the necessities for their own inner health and strength; but they add up to much the same conclusions. Many of the most pressing problems of national and world ecumenism can be worked out most promisingly and most hopefully at the grass roots; thus local councils of churches have a great responsibility for service beyond their own immediate orbits. But the necessities of their own interior health point to the same obligations.

In summary, our day cries for the clear envisioning, and then the resolute achievement, of a new stage in the advance of Christian unity that brings our eyes sharply to focus upon the life of Christians and their churches in local communities—the realization of "grass-roots ecumenicity"—of worthy and effective Christian unity *here,* where Christ's people live and work and where they will fulfill or deny the reality of their membership within the one church of Christ, the true church of Christ. The ecumenical imperative for tomorrow is to bring the fact of Christian unity more fully and worthily to realization here—in villages and towns and cities. The goal of the ecumenical imperative for tomorrow is nothing less than: the demonstration within communities of the reality of the body of Christ.

Happily, *this* is an ecumenical imperative with direct and immediate meaning for every single Christian, whether minister or layman, however humble his status within the church of Christ, however limited his contacts with the wider and larger world Christian movement. For ordinary church folk, one of the frustrating features of ecumenical Christianity has been that it has seemed to them to have its existence on planes, global or national, far removed from their firsthand knowledge and experience. They might fervently but futilely wish that they could *go to* the ecumenical movement. The most many of them might hope for was that someday, somehow, they might enjoy the privileged opportunity of attendance, as a spectator if not as a vocal voting member, at some ecumenical gathering.

Well, all that is now reversed. The ecumenical movement has *come to* them. They are its most important participants because they themselves are destined to determine its future. If it be true that the whole ecumenical development can go forward in health and in strength only as it takes secure rootage and achieves healthy growth in unnumbered local communities of every size and type all over the world, then every Christian who recognizes that fact and responds to its individual call to him with conviction, dedication, and resolute determination stands on the front line of ecumenical advance.

A radically altered recognition of the significance of local ecumenicity and a no less drastic reconception and reordering of local ecumenicity carries us at once back to the larger and even more basic issue—the proper role of local councils of churches within national councils of churches and of national councils of churches within the World Council of Churches.

Here what we confront is an even more patent and grave anomaly. Councils of churches, as their names imply, are associations of churches, i.e., denominations, and are constituted primarily (in the case of the American National Council of Churches) or exclusively (in the case of the World Council of Churches) of officially designated representatives of the member churches and function under their direction. But the *programs* of these councils cannot be carried out with adequate effectiveness by their member churches alone but only by subordinate councils of churches—in the case of the World Council through national councils, in the case of a national council through local councils. Yet the latter bodies have no adequate recognized places in the *structures* of the superior councils whose work they execute.

Within the National Council of Churches U.S.A., this anomaly has been a matter of troubled attention and sharp debate for a number of years, and provision has been made for token indirect representation of local ecumenicity in the structure of the National Council through the intermediate level of state councils of churches but not in dimensions that accurately reflect the importance of local councils in the actual functioning of the National Council. Heretofore these representatives have been designated by the state councils, subject to the approval of the churches to which they severally belong. But, through revisions in the National Council Constitution adopted by its Assembly in December, 1960, henceforth such appointments will be made by the member churches of the National Council from lists nominated to it by state councils in consultation with local councils in their areas. This appears as a small change in procedure, but it is one that will have the effect of further removing state and local councils from direct representation and of further solidifying the principle that all elections to the National Council's Assembly and General Board shall be directly by denominations.

In the World Council, national councils of churches appear only "in association," that is, in a purely consultative capacity. But the World Council must depend increasingly upon these national council "associates" for the implementation of its work. Moreover, the present relationship of national councils to the World Council is the more anomalous because the latter is the world expression of the same form of church life, a council of churches.

To put the matter positively, both world and national councils rest *functionally* upon two corporate legs, two sets of bodies—member churches *and* subordinate councils of churches. But in the World Council, *membership* consists solely of member churches, in the American National Council preponderantly of member churches.

The functional anomaly is all too obvious. However, more is involved than bringing formal structure into accord with actual operation. At stake also is a theological issue—the ecclesiological significance of councils of churches. What is the theological as well as the functional significance of councils of churches within the church of Christ? This question can best be considered on the world level: the relation of *world interdenominationalism* and *world denominationalism*.[9]

This is one of the most important issues in the proposed integration of the World Council of Churches and the International Missionary Council. For, as we have said, the World Council is a fellowship of *churches*, i.e., denominations; but the International Missionary Council is a fellowship of *councils*, councils of missionary societies in lands of the older churches and national Christian councils in younger church areas. The Plan of Integration proposes to preserve the present structure of the International Missionary Council within an enlarged World Council of Churches through a Commission and Division on World Mission and Evangelism in which national Christian councils and missionary councils will have their place not as consultative "associates" but as constituent members.[10]

Is this still one more instance of *Christian missions* as the pathfinder for a larger and more authentic *Christian unity?*

iii

Clear across the earth and at almost every level, advance in interdenominational collaboration has been followed by resurgent denominationalism. The growth of world ecumenism and its organizational expression in the several world ecumenical bodies has resulted, albeit unwittingly and unwillingly, in the emergence of world confessionalism or, as it is sometimes misnamed, "ecumenical denominationalism."

The relation of world interdenominationalism and world denominationalism concerns the Christian world mission and the movement for Christian unity equally. Indeed, this is a concern that they hold in common and on which united thought and a uniform policy are urgently needed.

What is taking place is a story all too familiar in Christian history.

Indeed, it is important to recall that this is not the first instance of this paradoxical cause-and-effect sequence in the modern period. It has occurred at least twice before within the past century and a half, as a direct consequence of the rise of the two earlier and most powerful outpourings of spiritual vitality within Christendom in modern times, the two developments that were

[9] See pp. 127 ff.
[10] See Appendix II, pp. 186 ff.

the principal precursors and source springs of present-day ecumenical Christianity—Christian missions and the student Christian movements.

As recorded above, the events most generally recognized as marking the beginning of the modern missionary impulse toward Christian unity on either side of the Atlantic were the founding of the London Missionary Society in 1795 and of the American Board of Commissioners for Foreign Missions in 1810. And we have noted that neither was, strictly speaking, "interdenominational" but rather "nondenominational." Each owed its origin to *individual Christians* of different communions, not to official action of their church bodies. But for a number of years, each served as the agency through which several denominations discharged their missionary obligations and dispatched missionaries for service abroad. The later effect of each, however, was to quicken within these denominations a deepening conviction of missionary responsibility prompting them to initiate missionary societies within their respective Churches. Ultimately, both the London Missionary Society and the American Board virtually lost their original nondenominational character as one after another of the participating denominations created its own mission board, withdrew from interdenominational co-operation and threw its strength into its own missionary society. As Dr. Richey Hogg has pointed out, "With rising denominational consciousness and vigor in the nineteenth century, most of this co-operation was surrendered."[11]

Again, toward the end of the nineteenth century, fresh vitality flowed into the churches and the missionary enterprise through the birth of the student Christian movements They, likewise, were not interdenominational but rather *non*denominational in character, sponsored and supported by individual Christians of many communions but not initially by the churches themselves. Again, the earlier pattern was re-enacted: the example of the pioneering nondenominational student movements goaded the denominations to launch student work of their own; witness the burgeoning Wesley and Westminster Foundations, Luther, Canterbury, and Pilgrim Societies, etc., in the United States and the present trend toward world denominational student organizations. And again, as denominations imitated the Christian associations by sponsoring rival student societies, strength was sapped

11 Hogg, *op. cit.*, p. 14.

from the nondenominational pathfinders with palpable and lamentable weakening not only of ecumenical experience and training but also of the prophetic vision and pioneering effort that had been generated within the nondenominational fellowships.[12]

It might have been forecast, therefore, that the rise of the world-wide movement for Christian unity of these latter years would quickly lead to accentuated denominational consciousness, organization, and activity on a world scale. Just this has happened. The relation of "world confessionalism" to both the world mission and the World Council presents one of the most baffling problems, if not threats, to ecumenical Christianity.

From this historic pattern, now thrice repeated, what lessons may be drawn? First, contrary to common assumption, the pioneering advances of the Christian cause in modern times have not sprung from revitalized churches; the cause-and-effect relationship has been the reverse. Second, in due time the denominations have imitated the ecumenical example. Third, the domestication within the denominations of impulses that were initially nondenominational has, generally speaking, broadened the scope but diminished the prophetic vision and power of these impulses. Fourth, resurgent denominationalism, whether in missions or among students or in the life of the churches, has tended to sap the vitality, dull the cutting edge, and retard the fulfillment of true ecumenism.

This is an issue that, at the moment, is most painfully recognized and is being most actively canvassed within Christian unity discussions. Actually, it poses problems that are in their incidence even more central and in their outcome far more determinative for the world mission. Indeed, it may well be that sound solution within the Christian unity wing of ecumenical Christianity can be achieved only as the issues are first faced and rightly resolved among the younger churches.

To put the point bluntly: throughout large and ever-expanding areas of the world mission, and these on the whole the most

12 To be sure, the denominational student groups joined the earlier nondenominational Christian associations in what is now called the National Student Christian Federation, and four denominational student organizations —Disciples of Christ, Evangelical United Brethren, United Church of Christ, and United Presbyterian—entered into organic union in 1960 as the United Campus Christian Fellowship.

mature and prophetic, world denominationalism, far from being a logical and natural development in this era of world-consciousness, is an utter anachronism, a historical absurdity, an attempt to revive on a world scale a species already extinct and reverently but happily interred within these areas. What is the meaning of world confessionalism to the membership of United Churches of Christ, whether in Japan or in South India or in North India or in the Philippines or in China as well as in Canada and the United States? Is not participation in the world confessional bodies something like the deference, dutiful and not without its sentimental nostalgia, which we all pay to the family connection to which we owe our ancestry and which may have furnished us our name—"McLeod" or "Jones" or "Schmidt" or what-have-you? Is not presence at their periodic meetings somewhat like attendance at "gatherings of the clan" or similar "family conclaves," delightful if rather irrelevant, amusing even if a trifle boring?

The Amsterdam Assembly provided an interesting bit of evidence on this point. One evening was given over to world denominational meetings. By general report, almost without exception these gatherings were dull, wearisome, and fruitless. But there was one exception. It was the gathering of delegates from "united churches." That was live, thrilling, and immensely valuable. More than that; it was clear proof to those who were present that their true spiritual affinities as well as their practical concerns lie with sister united churches rather than with the denominations of their ancestry.

Clearly, what is at stake in this issue is, in the long view, the pattern of the church of Christ of the future. Concretely, shall the united churches of Christ that have already taken form in half a dozen of the most advanced younger church areas be acknowledged as forerunners of the normative Christian church of tomorrow? Or shall the pattern of historic denominationalism through the instrumentality of world organizations halt the multiplication of normative churches throughout the world and even, though doubtless not deliberately, strain if not shake the existing pathfinders?

Parenthetically, in considering this whole matter, it is important to hold in mind a factor that lies beneath the concrete and immediate issues of denominationalism vs. interdenominationalism and influences them vitally. This is the inherent logic

of polarity in human thought and life, to which we called attention earlier,[13] that makes it almost inevitable that an epoch of
ardent transdenominational exploration and achievement should
be followed by a reaction toward recovery and revival of denominational awareness and loyalty. In this intangible, largely un-
controllable, but seemingly inexorable tidal oscillation, may lie
the greatest threat to ecumenical advance in the coming days.
And not for the movement for Christian unity only, but hardly
less—indeed, perhaps far more—for the Christian world mission.

In any event, here is one of the most pressing of all current issues for ecumenical Christianity at every level—the right relation
between denominational and interdenominational church structures. Obviously, this is a matter to be thought through rightly
only in terms of the doctrine of the church. What *is* the normative conception of the body of Christ? At once, we are brought
within the orbit of fundamental theological questions, more particularly precisely the issues that are presently preoccupying
Faith and Order studies.

By a strange paradox of history, that issue which might be expected to be fundamental to all Christian unity discussions and
prior to all others has, until quite recently, been almost wholly
bypassed. It is the question: What is the ideal unity of Christ's
church? What is the nature of the unity to be sought? Not until
the Faith and Order consultation at Oberlin in the United States
in the summer of 1958 was that question lifted in ecumenical
consideration for major attention. And the Oberlin consultation,
valuable as were its discussions and conclusions on many matters,
cast virtually no definitive light on the theme that the gathering
was summoned to examine—"The Nature of the Unity We
Seek." (See Note at end of this Part, p. 149.)

To be sure, for great numbers of churchmen, the nature of the
unity of the church in its ideal realization is not an open question. Christian unity means membership within one institution,
the church of Christ. Indeed, a major difficulty in achieving an
ecumenical consensus in the matter is precisely the extent to
which those who hold this conception tend to regard it as axio-
matic, underestimating when they do not disregard the numbers
and strength of conviction of fellow Christians who reject what
seems to them beyond question. They assume that, in due time,

13 See pp. 98 f.

all Christians will "return" to the only valid conception of the unity of the church, i.e., their conception.

This is not the view only of those who come from one or another of the "catholic" branches of the church. One of the most brilliant ecumenical theologians and statesmen, Bishop Lesslie Newbigin, espouses the same certitude with spirited insistence:

> The common use of the phrase "spiritual unity" to refer to something which is understood to be preferable to corporeal unity, something indeed which makes corporeal unity unnecessary, is totally irreconcilable with the teaching of the New Testament. . . . The unity of the Church is of its essence. That unity is a spiritual unity. It is also a corporeal unity. . . . Nothing could more completely reverse the meaning of the New Testament insistence on the spiritual nature of the Church's unity than to say that it meant that visible, corporeal unity was of secondary importance. . . . There is one Spirit, and it follows that there is one Body.[14]

As Bishop Newbigin argues, this conception of the nature of Christian unity grounds itself upon what it believes to be unequivocal New Testament teaching, especially that of Paul in his exhortations in First Corinthians and Ephesians. This is not the place to examine the validity of this New Testament interpretation. It is sufficient to query whether Paul ever envisioned a "visible, corporeal unity" of the kind that is in the minds of those who look toward a single institutional church of Christ as the ideal for the corporate life of his followers on earth. It has been well said that Paul's thought moves between the "congregation" and the church universal, the "body of Christ." The main point is: this conception and the Biblical interpretation upon which it is based are unequivocally rejected by a large *and steadily increasing* proportion of the most ardent devotees of Christian unity.

Indeed, there are four principal alternative views of the ideal unity of Christ's church:[15]

1. The unity of *fellowship*. "The unity of the church is a spirit-

[14] Lesslie Newbigin, *The Reunion of the Church* (S.C.M. Press, Ltd., London, 1948), pp. 50–54.

[15] "Assembly Document 1" in preparation for the World Council's Third Assembly recognizes *three* "types of unity" which correspond roughly to "2," "3," and "4," below, although the order of the last two is reversed. More important, the Assembly paper's third type ("3," below) does not so much as mention the expression of this form of Christian unity in conciliar association which is our main concern at this point.

ual unity; outward unity of organization is not of the essence of the church; true Christians are in fact united already."[16]

2. The unity of *"mutual recognition,"* involving a free interchange of memberships and ministries and full intercommunion between the several Christian churches, however numerous and varied they may be. According to this view, the ideal will have been achieved when Christians, whether lay or clerical, while holding membership in some particular branch of the church as they do in a particular congregation, will be universally recognized by all Christians of whatever branch of the church on a basis of full equality.

3. The unity of *association* in fellowship and co-operative action, involving full "mutual recognition," to be sure, but not exhausted by mutuality of recognition. In this view, numerous existing councils of churches culminating in the World Council are imperfect anticipations of the ultimate unity of the church, imperfect mainly in that full mutual recognition of the member churches by one another has not yet been achieved.

4. The unity of complete *corporate* or *organic union.* This is the "catholic" view already mentioned.

Within the ecumenical movement, choice lies between the latter two of the four possibilities. These are the alternative conceptions of the ideal unity of Christ's church—conciliar association *or* corporeal union. The case for the latter is fully understood and has thus far tended to dominate ecumenical discussion.

Those who find their ideal of Christian unity fulfilled in *conciliar association* rather than *visible institutional union*[17] argue mainly along these lines:

1. Theirs, they contend, is closer to the New Testament conception of the body of Christ—"unity of the Spirit in the bond of peace."

2. This was, in fact, the nature of the church's unity throughout the early centuries, a unity of mutual recognition that found an agency for common voice and corporate action through periodic church councils. This is still, both in theory and in practice, the ruling conception within Eastern Orthodoxy—the association of autocephalous churches in ecumenical fellowship and

16 Newbigin, *op. cit.,* p. 24. Bishop Newbigin himself rejects this view.

17 "Corporeal" union does not resolve the problem, since that connotes a "living" union that may be far more authentic and vital within a church council than in a single church structure.

council. The alteration of this primitive and early conception of the church's unity in favor of the conception of a single ecclesiastical structure should be recognized, it is maintained, as a perversion wrought mainly by the Church of Rome and influenced in no small measure by the parallel development of the political structure of one Holy Roman Empire.

3. This pattern of Christian unity alone can adequately provide for the rich varieties in Christian experience, worship, and organization that God has in fact brought to birth in the history of the church and which he intends should continue to enrich the universal church.

4. This pattern of Christian unity alone can safeguard Christians and their churches against the ever-present menace of overlarge, too powerful ecclesiastical organization with its well-nigh unfailing corollary of overbearing clerical hierarchy.

Again, it is not our purpose to adjudicate between these alternative views. It is important to recognize that here is an unsettled issue of quite major moment. And it is a point of division among Christians that grows more rather than less acute as the proportion of Christians who hold firmly to the "noncatholic" position becomes steadily larger.

It must be recognized that conciliar ecumenicity itself, through the official declarations of the World Council and the imitative voices of national and local councils of churches, has lent some support to the assumption that the ideal unity of Christ's church is one of organic or institutional union.

No declaration of the World Council has been repeated more frequently or more insistently than that the World Council is not, cannot be, and has no intention of becoming "a superchurch." This was anticipated by the Amsterdam Assembly. It was reiterated in fuller exposition at Toronto in 1950 in the authoritative document "The Church, the Churches, and the World Council of Churches." As the General Secretary has often declared: "The role of the [World] Council is merely instrumental. It must decrease in order that the Una Sancta may increase."[18] These disclaimers are often extended to the declaration that a council of churches not only is not "the church"; it is not "a church." The time has come when the adequacy of this declaration requires scrutinizing.

A council of churches is certainly not *the* church. But, then,

18 Rouse and Neill, *op. cit.,* p. 722.

neither is any one of the existing ecclesiastical bodies—communions, denominations, sects—in the present divided state of the body of Christ.

Can it be said with equal positiveness and without qualification that a council of churches is not *a* church?

The assumption behind this disclaimer is that the denomination *is* the church. Dr. Truman Douglass well characterizes this as the "denominational presupposition—the uncritical assumption that the denomination and its enterprises are proper objects of ultimate loyalty."[19]

But *is* the denomination the church of Christ? Is it, in any profound and authentic sense, more nearly the church of Christ than a council of churches? The denominational presupposition rests its claim that the denomination *is* the church of Christ upon one or more of three grounds: (*a*) The denomination has a common history and tradition. (*b*) The denomination is united by a common body of doctrine or creed. (*c*) The denomination ordains a ministry and administers sacraments.

As to the first—*a common history and tradition*—it is obviously true that most of the denominations can claim a lengthier history, a more hoary tradition, than can councils of churches. And yet, in the larger perspective of Christian history, every one of the denominations is a relatively latecomer. Each was initially a "sect," a "splinter group"; each was and is schismatic from the true church of Christ. Moreover, relative antiquity is no guarantee of authenticity.

As to the second—*a common body of doctrine*—if there is a single finding that stands forth with indisputable clarity from more than two decades of ecumenical examination and debate regarding the creedal bases of our existing denominations, it is this: on the basic issues of Christian belief (excepting only the doctrine of the church) there are no determinative differences between denominations. As the Edinburgh Faith and Order Conference of 1937, summarizing the essential beliefs of Christian faith under the caption "The Grace of Our Lord Christ," declared: "We agree on the following statement and recognize that there is in connection with this subject *no ground for maintaining division between Churches.*"[20] The same startling conclusion is

19 *Ibid.*
20 *Faith and Order,* Edinburgh, 1937, p. 224. On this whole matter, see the much fuller discussion in my *World Christianity: Yesterday, Today, and Tomorrow,* Ch. 8.

set forth even more explicitly in a report of a joint commission of
Anglican and Free Churchmen in Great Britain in 1950:

> On the doctrine of God the Father, the Person and Work of Christ,
> the Person and mission of the Holy Spirit, the Trinity and the Life
> Everlasting we have found nothing which separates any one of these
> Communions from another. (P. 115.)

More than that: the major theological divergences are *within* not
between denominations.

As to the third—*ministry and sacraments*—within the membership of the World Council and of many national and local
councils of churches are bodies (e.g., the Friends, the Salvation
Army) that do not ordain a ministry and do not celebrate sacraments.

Clearly what is at stake is the most basic question of all: *What,
where, and when is the church of Christ?* Let us put that question
to the test of concrete illustration.

When the World Council of Churches meets in Assembly at
Amsterdam or Evanston or New Delhi, are we at liberty to say
that it is less truly and fully the church of Jesus Christ than when
the bishops of the Anglican Communion gather at Lambeth, or
the Lutheran World Federation meets in Minneapolis, or the adherents of the Reformed tradition assemble in Brazil?

When members of a dozen or a score or a hundred and fifty
Christian "churches" partake of the sacrament of Holy Communion in ecumenical fellowship, is this less fully and truly a
celebration of the Supper of Jesus Christ than when a larger or
smaller number of Christ's disciples from one or another of the
severed limbs of his church partake of his body and blood according to the rites of their denomination?

For many Christians, these questions are immediately and
categorically answered in the affirmative. But there are others who
find themselves compelled to face these same questions in a
slightly different and what they cannot but regard as a more compelling perspective: If Jesus Christ himself were to come among
us today, would he recognize a Presbyterian or Methodist or
Anglican Church as his church, and deny that recognition to his
followers when they meet in common worship as fellow Christians
across and despite sectarian divisions? Would Christ recognize a
church council as less truly his church than one or another struc-
tural branch of that church? Does Christ accept as less truly a
partaking of his body and blood the sharing in Holy Communion
by representatives of many Christian churches than the ob-

servance of the sacrament by members of one particular "church"?

These are the questions that stand at the heart of the confrontation of ecumenism and denominationalism. They are questions that are genuinely *new,* without precedent in the previous history of Christendom. They are new because they are created by a new form of churchly reality, of Christian community, which has come to birth within Christendom in our own time and which has been blessed by God with amazing growth and strength in these latter years—what is sometimes spoken of as "conciliar ecumenicity"—Christian councils and councils of churches, of which the World Council of Churches is the climactic and supreme illustration.

It is doubtful whether there is any other issue that is more pregnant for the future of the church of Christ and therefore more clamant upon the attention and action of the responsible leaders of that church than precisely the achievement of the right relationship between this new form of churchly reality, "conciliar association," and the denominational structures that have come to us as a legacy of past Christian centuries.

As we have already noted, this is an issue that has been forced upon the ecumenical consciousness in concrete illustration in the joining of the two world Christian bodies that ground themselves respectively upon the two alternative forms of churchly reality. Here is not the least significance in the imminent "integration" of the International Missionary Council and the World Council of Churches.

We have considered the role of Christian councils in relation to historic denominational structures in terms of the doctrine of the church. But if the "crisis" confronting the world Christian movement is really as novel and as urgent as we have suggested, there is also required a radical re-examination of the role and functioning of councils in the strategy of ecumenical Christianity in responding to the pressing demands upon it.

This issue has been exposed with brilliant clarity and devastating candor in one of the most radical (in the authentic and laudatory sense of "getting to the roots of things"), most penetrating as it is certainly most provocative, and most important utterances concerning ecumenical Christianity in the past decade —Dr. Truman Douglass' paper entitled "Our Co-operative Witness to Our Oneness in Christ."[21]

21 *Op. cit.*

In the passage quoted earlier, Dr. Douglass proposes:

> We are in need of a reinterpretation of the meaning of interchurch co-operation that will provide a basis for assigning to councils of churches responsibilities and tasks which are of the highest moment for the mission of the church. Our present arrangement is one in which the denominations are likely to retain for themselves most of the exhilarating opportunities for Christian action. The tasks delegated to the councils tend to be either ecclesiastically unprofitable functions, such as ministries to migrants and Indians, or the kind of errands that can only be classified as religious and ethical trivialities. I think the most disastrous consequence of this policy is that in the minds of millions of Americans, councils of churches have become identified with a thoroughly depressing kind of moralism.

Dr. Douglass is writing within the context of the American scene and with his thought focused upon local ecumenicity. But much of what he has to say applies almost equally at the national and world levels.

In our examination of local ecumenicity, we made bold to declare: "Not one of the community evils crying for elimination can be effectively mitigated, not one of the advances crying for implementation can be significantly furthered by individual congregations or single denominations—not one."

If this is true of the witness and work of the church of Christ within communities, it is not one whit less true of the witness and work of the church in nations and across the world.

This is true of the churches' impact on the world of nations. In a world crying for the healing of its divisions, and breaking to pieces for lack of it, the churches of Christ have no right to rebuke the nations for their disunity, or to expect to exert a significant influence—and they certainly will not in fact do so—so long as they perpetuate in their own beings the very infections of disorder and division that require cure.

It is no less true of the churches in America. Those churches cannot bring an effective impact upon any one of the great problem areas or pioneering tasks—the halting of secularism, the confrontation of government, the reclamation of education, the Roman Catholic problem, outreach and occupation, the social order—unless they act unitedly with every resource at their pooled command.

Thirty years ago, that great prophet of a united Christendom, the late Bishop Charles H. Brent, cried out: "The world is too strong for a divided church!" Well, let us face the fact: every city in this and every country, every nation on earth, the world of nations, is too strong for a divided church. We repeat: to each major problem confronting the churches, to every one of the church's most urgent tasks, there is only one adequate answer: the massed strength of all churches directed unitedly upon common responsibilities. Christian unity is, first of all, the clear counsel of expediency, of practical statesmanship.

On the other hand, unity is laid upon the churches as an inescapable obligation by the command of Christ. Their present state is a denial of their own faith; it is blatant disloyalty to the clear direction of him whom they acknowledge as master. Unity is, then, finally and decisively, a matter of elementary fidelity to the churches' basic commission from Christ and to his expectation of them.

Let us be quite clear what is the Christian unity that is required. So far as the world Christian movement is vital at all, it is like a living organism. As with any other organism, individual or corporate, it is determined by laws of health that are not created by it but "given" to it. To disobey those laws is to sicken and die. The most obvious and obdurate of those controlling the Christian mission is—the imperative to growth. This it shares with all other organisms in the phase of their youth and vitality. In God's world there is no standing still. There is only advance or regression. This is true of the moral life, both of persons and of their societies. We must go higher or we shall go lower. "He that is not with us is against us." Over the long years, the individual or group that will not obey the given laws for its own growth stagnates, then deteriorates, and finally degenerates; it slips or is swept aside; the currents of advance pass over or around it, and go on.

Moreover, the inexorables of health are not only in the given conditions of existence. Organisms, by the fashion in which they grow, create an *inner* logic for their own further development; advance *must be* in accord with, and in fulfillment of, the previous pattern of development.

The advance in Christian unity so graphically suggested by the contrast between a century and a half ago and today has not been achieved by a single jump or by a gradual escalatorlike ascent along an unbroken line upward. It has been achieved by a sequence of clearly distinguishable steps, each successive step being the necessary sequel to its predecessor, but all together constituting a continuous development. To take a parallel from a very primitive level, the world Christian movement is less like an amoeba than a chambered nautilus. In each case, the organism grows imperceptibly in accordance with the given laws of health. But the amoeba has no structure beyond its own flabby, unprotected, perilously fragile self. The chambered nautilus also develops imperceptibly, but its safety for growth is secured by its shell; and its growth requires that, periodically, it make for itself a new shell, adequate for its enlarging body, and leave the former encasement that has served it well but has now become too constricted, a threat of death rather than an aid to life. This is the logic of advance for all societies. The *organism* itself grows gradually, in accordance with the given laws of health. But the *structure* that sustains and safeguards it, making possible its further development, must be changed from time to time; and that change is less by imperceptible development than by radical displacement.

For the world Christian movement, that has been the inner logic of advance this past century and a half—not unbroken, effortless movement, but step-by-step advance, in which the achievement and glory of each successive step sinks into sterility and futility save as it is fulfilled in and replaced by the next fated and necessary leap.

For some years it has been clearly apparent that the growing organism was suffering increasing and enfeebling constriction in the once-glorious structure of comity and co-operation. If one may force the figure, certain limbs of the organism have already created new and more adequate shells for themselves, while the parent body strains within the old pattern. As we would expect, advance to the next stage of Christian unity occurred first in the outreaching tentacles of the organism on the mission field, just because there vitality is strongest, growth fastest, structure most supple, the inner necessity for new and more adequate patterns most insistent. Union institutions—in higher education, in medicine, in theological training—are cases in point. Here, as we noted earlier, in contrast to the stage of co-operation, resources are pooled, forces are joined, not merely in planning and in producing the instruments for each church's separate work (Bibles, Christian literature), but for the actual prosecution of a specialized segment of the work itself. And in at least five areas—Iraq, Nepal, Portugal, the Copper Belt in Northern Rhodesia, and the

Andean mountains of Ecuador—United Missions, embracing the
missionary programs of several denominations, have been created.
These new structures required by life developments in the
tentacles have had response, sometimes tardily, at a corresponding
part of the parent organism, for example, in America in the
United Board for Christian Higher Education in Asia, and in
joint boards to match united missions or fully union churches—
for Japan, the Philippines, South India, Okinawa, Santo Domingo, the Upper Nile, Hong Kong, and elsewhere. We may
name this stage *confederation*. It connotes fully united programs
of operation, though without surrender of final authority and responsibility by the separate constituents.

However, growth of the organism continues apace. Clearly, the
prevailing structure—so novel, so ample, so liberating when first
formed—begins to pinch, to limit, to inhibit, at some points to
strangle, the advance of life. A cycle of growth is completing its
course again. The inner logic for health once again imposes inexorable demands. The nautilus of the world Christian movement cries for a new shell, new structures, more nearly matched
to the vital realities and promise of the living organism itself.

What should be its character? The impatient, those who dis-
cern the trend of advance but not its step-by-step logic, those who
envision the ultimate goal but not the tedious stairway toward its
achievement, cry for instant and complete organic union of our
churches—or, in any event, of their mission boards. We should
be guided less by obedience to a priori conceptions describing
what someday should be than by discernment of the inner logic
of growth prescribing what today must be. Those enamored of
the far-off divine event all too readily evade the near and instant
divine imperative. Not organic union of all the churches, but an
obligation far more immediate and immediately achievable is
the divine imperative to us today.

How shall we identify this next stage, this new shell now required to serve the nautilus? It is easier to illustrate its specifications than to coin its title. For the latter, perhaps the most accurate designation is *functional union*. What is next required is
the development for the entire organism of the pattern already
improvised under necessity for its most vigorous and pioneering
tentacles; the extension to the world Christian movement as a
whole of the structure and practice now tried and proved in

union Christian higher education, medicine, theological training on the mission field, and in united boards at home.

However, one cannot extend the principle of advance from co-operation to confederation for the whole without more far-reaching change than is necessary for anticipatory developments in the parts. The world Christian movement should be recognized as at the stage in its organic development when, if it is to continue to advance and not stumble and halt with threat of stagnation and, in some areas and aspects, atrophy, it must *function as the world Christian movement*. It must function as one organic whole. And its shell, its structures, must be patterned by the demands of its emerging life and in full conformity to its requirements.

What, concretely, would this imply? We may suggest five specifications:

1. A *united strategy*—the planning of the entire world evangelistic enterprise of the churches as one organic movement, determined in the light of the total task and the total resources available.

2. A *united message*—the same message, unmistakably one, though spoken in a variety of tongues, as those of different languages and cultures and traditions utter the same, unmistakably the same, message.

3. A *united program*, made possible by the pooling of all resources—men and money—and their deployment according to a united plan for largest effectiveness.

4. A *united leadership*—the conscription of the ablest leaders out of every communion for the service of all the churches, the whole church, the one church.

5. A *united community*—fellowship, *koinōnia*—made possible by a commanding rededication in the face of one Christ and one world.

Yes, but more specifically, what changes in our present procedures and organizations are indicated? It would imply a fundamental shift of the center of gravity, the place of decision, the locus of responsibility. The same churches would participate, but in new relationships. The same persons would function, but in different patterns. The same resources—no, pray God, vastly augmented resources!—would be deployed in the service of the same objectives and in the same enterprises—yes, but, pray God, in many new enterprises also, and in different and far more worthy ways. It implies a shift of the center of gravity from individual churches or boards to one, or several, united boards. It means that the most important decisions will be taken together, in united conference, where each person, while still a denominational representative, is empowered by his church to think and act consciously and primarily for the whole church. It would mean that the staff and members of each church or board would spend more time, give more of their best thought, take more decisions of major import, actually function as servants of their church more, in and through united boards than in their present familiar patterns. It means that most of them, from time to time, and some of them for their whole time, would be drafted into full-time service of the united boards. Be clear: this does not mean they will cease to direct the enterprise of their own church. They will still be doing that work in accordance with the realities of its advancing life. They are not "on loan" from their own church for service in some rather nebulous interdenominational undertaking. They are at their own job *for* their own church in the most prophetic, strategic, and important projects it is furthering.

Among social organisms, the processes of growth lie largely, as they do in human organisms, within the mystery of Providence. But the *structures* that house each organism, that assure its perpetuation, that determine its further advance or its stagnation and, it may be, atrophy—these are man's creation.

In speaking of the rise of the ecumenical movement, Archbishop Temple said: "No human agency has planned this. . . . *God* has been building up a Christian fellowship which now extends into almost every nation, and binds citizens of them all together in true unity and mutual love." The unity now required is further evidence of the powerful working of a hand, not a human hand, in ecumenical Christianity. No other explanation is adequate. *God* has been building up an organism—the world Christian movement—throbbing with life, pregnant with power, far beyond the adequacy of the shell we have built as its home and its instrument. The charge comes:

"Build ye more worthy mansions, ye leaders of the world Christian movement."

In the ancient world it was said, "All roads lead to Rome." In contemporary politics, all questions end in Moscow. In the life of the Christian churches in our age, every problem and every responsibility points to a single inexorable necessity—Christian unity.

Nothing less than the whole church of Christ will suffice for the needs of the hour, or satisfy the churches' Lord.

iv

From the earliest informal conversations in the mid-thirties, exploring the possibility and desirability of creating a world Christian body officially representative of the churches, the relationship of such a body to the Christian World Mission and its agency, the International Missionary Council, was in the forefront of attention.

This was inevitable, if for no other reason in view of the solid fact of history that has furnished the starting point of this book that the modern ecumenical development in almost every one of its many and varied aspects had its origin within the missionary enterprise. As we noted, the Edinburgh World Missionary Conference of 1910 led to the creation not only of the International Missionary Council as its direct outcome but hardly less, as an indirect result, to the Faith and Order Movement, one of the two parents of the World Council of Churches; its influence in preparing the way for the Life and Work Movement, the other parent of the World Council, was almost as great. It is a truism that the World Mission was both the precursor and the progenitor of the World Council.

Moreover, almost without exception the men majorly instrumental in the bringing to birth of the World Council—Archbishop William Temple, Dr. William Adams Brown, Dr. J. H. Oldham, Dr. William Paton, Dr. W. A. Visser 't Hooft, to name only a few—were deeply committed to the World Mission and had had their vision of Christian unity quickened if not created through it. Those who have come late upon the ecumenical scene and are unfamiliar with its history sometimes assume that proposals for closer integration of the two world bodies originate with Christian unity "ecumaniacs" having meager appreciation of the significance of missions, that the World Council aims to "gobble up" the International Missionary Council. Actually, concern for the right relationship of these two major expressions of ecumenicity has been earliest and strongest among those whose initial loyalty was to missions. That concern has been twofold— on the one hand that the effort for Christian unity embodied in the World Council should be informed by the vision, dynamic, and commitment of Christian missions at its heart, and on the other hand that the world mission as represented by the International Missionary Council should not be crowded into the background by the newer and more officially ecclesiastical World Council of Churches.

Accordingly, from the first projection of the World Council, measures were devised to assure the fullest possible collaboration of the two bodies. At the time of the World Missionary Conference at Madras in December, 1938, six months after the drafting of the Constitution of the World Council and its submission to the churches, a joint committee was formed, and one of the senior secretaries of the International Missionary Council, Dr. William Paton, was appointed the first Associate General Secretary of the World Council.[22] The intervention of World War II and Dr. Paton's untimely death retarded the fulfillment of these intentions. But, with the end of the war, a sequence of specific steps has drawn the two Councils into ever more intimate and manifold co-operation. Each of these steps was taken, not in deference to some a priori conception, but as direct response to demands arising from the discharge of concrete tasks:

1. In 1946, less than a year after the conclusion of World War II and two years before the World Council formally came into being, the manifest need for an organ to guide and speak for the entire world Christian movement in the international scene led the two bodies to launch the Commission of the Churches on International Affairs (C.C.I.A.), which has served them both with ever-enlarging influence and effectiveness through the past decade.

2. At the time of the First Assembly of the World Council at Amsterdam in 1948, the two bodies voted formal "association" and modified their official titles to read:

THE WORLD COUNCIL OF CHURCHES

in association with

THE INTERNATIONAL MISSIONARY COUNCIL

and the obverse.

3. At the Bangkok conference sponsored jointly by the two Councils in 1949, they created a Joint East Asia Secretariat to represent them both in relationship to churches and missions throughout this vast subcontinent. Eight years later, this was

22 Compare Rouse and Neill, *op. cit.*, p. 706.

succeeded by the East Asia Christian Conference as a continuing body.

4. At the Willingen Assembly in 1952, the I.M.C. authorized the World Council's Division of Interchurch Aid to act for both in administering relief and emergency interchurch aid in Asia and Africa. As the area of I.C.A.'s operations has broadened to embrace the whole world and the scope of its activities extended from "emergency" relief to continuing interchurch service, the interest and participation of the I.M.C. in the I.C.A. have increased, with an appropriate enlargement of representation in its direction.

5. At the Second World Council Assembly at Evanston in 1954, the research and study programs of the two bodies were completely unified in a single *division of studies* within the World Council but serving both Councils.

6. At the same time, the Joint Committee was reconstituted, its mandate was redefined and enlarged to embrace "the study of the advantages, disadvantages, and implications of a full integration of the I.M.C. and the W.C.C."[23] and the Joint Committee was strengthened through the appointment of a full-time Secretary, Dr. Norman Goodall.

Thus, the undertakings in which the I.M.C. and the W.C.C. are presently joined in varied patterns account for a larger and larger part of the actual work of each body. Functional integration over wide areas is already an accomplished fact, passing far beyond what is implied in the formal relationship of "association."

Meanwhile, developments within each body compelled a fresh examination of their relationship. On the one hand, the historic missionary societies and boards that constitute the membership of the I.M.C. within older-church areas are increasingly servants of churches that are members of the W.C.C.; functionally and even structurally, they are missionary agencies of its member churches. On the other hand, not a few of the national Christian councils that furnish the membership of the I.M.C. among the younger churches have become also "associated councils" of the W.C.C. And as "missions" give way to "younger churches" and as the latter advance to maturity, they desire to take their places in both bodies. Thus, the constituency of the two bodies has become more

[23] Report of the Joint Committee at the Evanston Assembly. *The Evanston Report*, p. 322, W. A. Visser 't Hooft, editor. Harper & Brothers, 1955.

and more the same. But this involves a dual relationship and responsibility that, however enriching, is often confusing and burdensome.

More fundamental and more significant, the outlooks of the two bodies have been drawing closer and closer. When they were brought into "association" at Amsterdam, the hope was expressed that this relationship would deepen "the mission consciousness of churches and the church consciousness of missions." The past twelve years have witnessed a fulfillment of that hope beyond expectation. At the same time, many of their most pressing concerns and baffling perplexities are closely parallel if not identical —the problems of religious liberty and proselytism, of evangelism in the face of secularism, nationalism and non-Christian faiths, of relationships with Christian churches beyond "the curtains" and with powerfully evangelistic groups outside the ecumenical fellowship, etc. Their responsible officers find it natural and appropriate, indeed inescapable, to think and plan and act together, as though the two bodies that they respectively represent were already one. And, in all these respects, there is an unmistakable acceleration in the process of growing together, due less to deliberate design than to an inherent and inexorable inner logic.

However, the major imperative toward a closer integration of the two movements, and their respective world organs, lies at a deeper, a theological, level. It was first voiced in the report of the Central Committee of the World Council at its discussions at Rolle in the summer of 1951, in which officers of the International Missionary Council had an influential voice, on "The Calling of the Church to Mission and to Unity" and was rephrased by the Joint Committee in the introduction to its recommendations for integration:

> The main concern of the two Councils must be the total task of the Church in the world. That task includes both the witness of the Church to the ends of the earth and the concern for the manifestation of the unity of the body of Christ.

> The *unity* of the Church and the *mission* of the Church both belong, in equal degree, to the *essence* of the Church. . . . This truth has already become manifest in the life of both world bodies. It has led them into association with each other and now obliges them to go farther.

It had long been recognized that all this points toward the day when the possibility of still closer relationship, perhaps complete unification, of the two Councils should receive serious consideration. Indeed, as we have just observed, when the Joint Committee, their over-all consultative agency, was reconstituted in 1954, it was specifically charged "to study the advantages, disadvantages, and implications of a full integration of the International Missionary Council and the World Council of Churches." The considerations outlined above are among those which led the Joint Committee at its meeting in 1956 to recommend to its parent bodies that the time for a fresh examination of these questions had arrived and to request permission to prepare a draft plan for possible integration. That permission was granted, and the Joint Committee began its task "in the fullest possible consultation with all concerned."

In view of what we have ventured to term "an inherent and inexorable inner logic" drawing the two world movements into ever closer, more intricate and (as many would hold) enriching mutual involvement, query may naturally arise in the minds of many as to why complete unification has been so long delayed. Such questioning is likely to be particularly insistent and perhaps impatient among those who witnessed a closely parallel integration of the Foreign Missions Conference within the National Council of Churches in the United States in 1950, with what many consider notable strengthening of the missionary consciousness and conviction of the American churches. A special obligation has rested upon them not to view the world problem through American spectacles, but to come into an informed and sympathetic understanding of the disquiet with which the proposed "integration" has been contemplated in certain quarters.

In the first place, there are differences in the organizational structures of the two world movements which, some hold, reflect contrasts in principle and philosophy with profound spiritual significance. As we have more than once pointed out, the World Council is a council of *churches;* its membership consists wholly of ecclesiastical bodies with their perils of clericalism, sacerdotalism, and theological and organizational rigidity and conservatism. The International Missionary Council is a council of *councils;* as just noted its membership is made up from councils of missionary societies in the West and national Christian councils in younger-church lands.

In many countries, the missionary societies have originated

outside of, if not in spite of, the traditional churches. They are an expression of the voluntary devotion of groups of individual Christians of prophetic vision and missionary consecration who distrust the limiting and deadening hand of ecclesiasticism. They regard with misgiving the increasingly prevailing American pattern of missions as simply an expression of the concern and responsibility of churches. They believe that the merger of the International Missionary Council with the World Council of Churches would not only fail to provide adequate influence for nonecclesiastical missionary groups but might also lose from the Christian World Mission the voluntary initiative that has so largely given it birth. They fear that the ultimate outcome would be a relegation of missions to peripheral inconsequence.

At the same time, the national Christian councils that have sprung up all over the world as the fruit of missions embody two priceless values that find no corresponding recognition within World Council structure. On the one hand, their memberships embrace not only churches but also freer Christian movements such as the Y.M.C.A. and Y.W.C.A., which have only a consultative status in the World Council. On the other hand, they express the natural and sound association of Christians and churches on national and regional bases, while in the World Council participation moves from individual member churches direct to the world body. They consider that the World Council's invitation to national church councils to become "associated councils" offers, at best, second-class participation in its life and work. In this contention they speak not only for Christians of younger-church areas but also for all who believe strongly in the vital role of local, regional, and national councils.

In all preliminary discussion of possible integration, these misgivings were at the center of consideration. The Joint Committee laid down the following *sine qua non* of an acceptable plan:

> The Committee regards it as imperative that any such integration should be in a form which ensures that missions belong to the heart of the ecumenical movement. It should also be on lines which bring the missionary forces into closer relationship with all phases of the church's witness in the life of the world and engage the fullest resources of the churches in the task of formulating and fulfilling their mission in terms commensurate with the needs of the world today and with the nature of the "glorious gospel of the blessed God."

The officers of the I.M.C. defined this precondition somewhat more explicitly as follows:

> Before proceeding to submit to its member councils any proposal for a possible integration of the two organizations, the I.M.C. must satisfy itself that the result would be to bring the missionary obligation of the church more sharply into focus as a central responsibility of the entire ecumenical movement, and not to relegate it to a peripheral status. . . . It must be assured that the actual plan of reorganization would promote this outcome, with such changes in the present structure and procedures of the W.C.C. as this would entail; changes which may be as radical and far-reaching for the W.C.C. as for the I.M.C. . . . There would be required provision for the necessary measure of autonomy for the missionary arm . . . and adequate representation of mission interests in the central bodies of the Council, and vice versa.

In summary, it is clear that two objects must be fulfilled:

1. The missionary conviction and commitment that are the very being of the International Missionary Council must permeate the entire life of the integrated Council and find appropriate recognition and effective voice in its structure—its Assembly and Central Committee as well as staff and working committees.

2. The life and program of the International Missionary Council in its full scope and strength must continue in undiminished power within the integrated Council.

The translation of these basic principles into terms of a specific plan was precisely the assignment that the Joint Committee, with wide consultation, undertook. Preliminary discussions took full account both of the general misgivings with respect to integration and of the specific conditions that would be required in an acceptable plan. These discussions revealed that there is not a single difficulty that cannot be met to the full satisfaction of virtually all representatives of both councils who have participated. Indeed, differences of judgment that remained were discovered to lie not between spokesmen of the two bodies but rather among the officers of each.

The Plan of Integration[24]

From the outset, it has been recognized that the Plan might move along either of two main alternative lines. There were

[24] This is given in full in Appendix II, pp. 186 ff.

advocates of each alternative within the Joint Committee. Both
were seriously and carefully considered.

1. One proposal envisaged the "disintegration" of the two
existing Councils and their replacement by a body substantially
new, perhaps with a new name.

The Joint Committee undertook detailed exploration of this
possibility not once but repeatedly in the course of its discussions
over two years and was finally led to its definite rejection. If we
were dealing with two pieces of organizational machinery, it
might be possible to break both down into their constituent elements and recast them in some wholly new pattern. But those are
not the realities to be joined. These two movements are living
organisms. It is the union of two living realities that must be
sought without loss of the vital values embodied in each.

2. In consequence, the Joint Committee was led over and over
again to the second alternative method of integration, which
would seek to conserve to the full all that is best in both movements and yet also open the promise of an enlarged and more
effective future. That goal, the plan seeks to assure. No figure
drawn from the vocabulary of organizational relationships, or
even of organic relationships, is adequate to indicate what is
attempted. "Merger" carries connotations from the realm of
business amalgamations. "Marriage" suggests an intimate but
still too external relationship. "Grafting" is, perhaps, the least
inadequate figure, if we hold steadily in view that it is two fully
formed living bodies that it is proposed to unite in a single
organism.

We have said that two objectives must be fulfilled: (a) The
missionary conviction and commitment which is the very being
of the International Missionary Council must permeate every
part of the integrated Council and find appropriate recognition
and effective operation in its entire life. (b) The life and program
of the International Missionary Council in its full scope and
strength must continue in undiminished power within the integrated Council. The Plan seeks to realize each of these two
purposes primarily through two steps, four in all.

The continuation of the present life and program of the International Missionary Council is to be secured through:

1. The creation of a *Commission on World Mission and Evangelism*. This is substantially the perpetuation within the integrated Council of the present Assembly of the International Mis-

sionary Council. "Its aim shall be to further the proclamation to the whole world of the gospel of Jesus Christ, to the end that all men may believe in him and be saved." The Commission will meet every five or six years in the intervals between meetings of the World Council Assembly. Its membership will be drawn preponderantly from the present member councils of the I.M.C. and other similar councils that may subsequently become affiliated with the Commission, supplemented by appointments by the Central Committee to assure representation from the full World Council constituency, including its present Department of Evangelism. "The Commission shall formulate general lines of policy and programme . . . for submission to the Central Committee for its approval."

2. The creation of a *Division of World Mission and Evangelism* that follows closely the plan of other World Council Divisions and thus brings the structure into harmony with the prevailing pattern of present World Council operation. The Division is the ad interim body responsible for "carrying out the aim and functions of the Commission."

The Joint Committee gave much thought to the other objective, which was named first—to assure that missions shall be at the heart of the entire life and work of the World Council. Here, likewise, two steps are proposed:

1. Provision for representation within the Assembly and Central Committee of the World Council of those from all parts of the world with special knowledge in the field of world mission and for continuous attention to relationships of mutual helpfulness with associated and affiliated councils that desire to avail themselves of the services of the integrated Council. (Councils may be "associated" with the World Council as presently provided, or "affiliated" to the Commission on World Mission and Evangelism, or may enjoy both relationships.)

2. Lastly, all divisional and departmental activities of the World Council are to be re-examined to assure that "the missionary aim of the Council as a whole shall find expression in the work of all its divisions and departments."

At St. Andrews, Scotland, in August, 1960, the Administrative Committee of the International Missionary Council, acting on authorization of the Ghana Assembly two and a half years earlier, took definitive action committing the I.M.C. to integration, and the Central Committee of the World Council voted to submit to its member churches the required constitutional amendments for adoption at the Council's forthcoming Assembly at New Delhi.

In presenting this Plan to the International Missionary Council and the World Council, the Joint Committee concluded its introduction to its report with this statement:

> No plan can by itself ensure the spiritual integration which is our deepest desire. This can only come as a gift of God. Nevertheless, this plan is submitted to the two world bodies in the conviction that its realization will represent a decisive step of obedience toward the fulfillment of the total task which the Lord has entrusted to the whole church.

If, as now appears highly probable, final approval of the Plan is given by the overwhelming majority of the constituencies of both Councils and the "integration" of the two Councils should be consummated in connection with the Third Assembly of the World Council scheduled for New Delhi in November, 1961, the outcome would be a single unified world Christian movement embracing the totality of ecumenical Christianity. Christian missions having preceded and so largely given birth to Christian unity, would then be embodied at the heart of the world body embracing both movements.

V

How, then, shall we appraise the significance of ecumenical Christianity for the troubled days ahead?

i

First of all, it is essential to assess at their full weight its very considerable limitations:

1. Ecumenical Christianity embraces only a part, though a very considerable part, of Christendom. From the roll of participant churches, there is one mighty and several other lesser but weighty absentees. Almost nothing that has been said of growing co-operation involves the Church of Rome, with a membership of roughly one half of Christendom. So long as Rome recognizes no

other body bearing the name of Christian as a true church and maintains a convinced and studied aloofness, there is no realistic prospect of participation by that church as a world body in ecumenical Christianity. Despite the interesting though still problematical proposal of the new Pope John XXIII for an "ecumenical council," there is no wisdom in cherishing illusions on that score.

Again, although many of the Eastern Orthodox communions have played an active role in earlier stages of the ecumenical development, the attitude of the Church of Russia, the largest and most influential Orthodox body, remains unsure. And, as in the political realm, Russia exerts a growing dominance over lesser Eastern Churches—Rumanian, Bulgarian, Estonian, Latvian, etc. Here, as in the affairs of nations, many uncertainties wait on one overarching question: What does Moscow intend?

2. In the second place, it must be conceded that participation in ecumenical Christianity is still largely confined to leaders of the several churches. Conviction of its importance, even awareness of its existence, has only begun to seep down into the rank-and-file membership. The great bulk of the life and work of the church is still in and through sectarian communions, unaware of the larger loyalty. Not until the movement has achieved grass rootage can it be said to be a movement of the Christians of the world; only then could its future be secure. On the other hand, it is not without significance that ecumenical Christianity does today claim the convinced allegiance and wholehearted support of most of the foremost leaders of its member churches.

3. Again, ecumenical Christianity, especially in its world organs, is still at the stage of first and modest beginnings. Measured in terms of financial resources, the budget placed annually at the disposal of the World Council of Churches for its regular work by nearly two hundred communions is less than the administrative expenditures for their own work of many of its member churches.

On the other hand, happily, financial strength is no measure whatever of spiritual effectiveness. Here, if anywhere, size of organization and budget are the poorest measuring rods. The guess may be hazarded—it is not subject to verification or disproof—that there is no place within the vast and intricate structure of world Christendom where each invested dollar is so economically husbanded and so productive of far-reaching spiritual results as in the meagerly furnished agencies of ecumenical Christianity.

4. Once more, it would be a mistake to exaggerate the influence of world Christianity upon the issues of public order and world peace. It cannot be too emphatically reiterated that the Christian church is not a political instrumentality pitting its strength against secular ideologies and governments. The influence it disseminates and the manner of its working are too gentle, too subtle to register clearly in the crude calculus of empire. Yet the churches are learning—and rapidly—that their ability to bring Christian insight and judgment to bear upon affairs of state is in direct proportion to the unity of their voice and action. And, it should be so. The churches cannot hope to heal the divisions of society—and they certainly will bring no significant healing or transforming power there—until they are cured of the disease of disunity and parochialism within their own organism. The church is, in principle, the expression of the spiritual reality and aspiration of the community, as the state is the expression of the community's political interests and concerns. If the community cannot show forth unity in spiritual purpose, how can it be expected to manifest political unity? This is true in every local community, in the nation, and in the world.

ii

On the other hand, three facts about ecumenical Christianity merit reflection:

1. First, it is something genuinely new, without precedent in the previous history of Christianity, or indeed of other social forces. Indeed, as we have noted, its emergence and advance represent a direct reversal of the tendencies toward schism and division that have dominated the Christian movement throughout its first eighteen centuries.

2. Second, although the first beginnings of the movement fell during that period when all the peoples of the earth were becoming conscious of one another, when powerful centripetal tides in world culture were parenting all manner of international associations and organizations so that superficially similar trends within the churches might plausibly have been read as a phase of general cultural drift, such an interpretation wholly fails to account for the steadily accelerating advance of Christian co-operation in the past two decades. Indeed, in the perspective of

cultural history, this may be the most notable, as it is certainly the most unexpected, fact: it is precisely while the community of peoples and nations was breaking asunder that the leaders of the Christian churches of the world have been drawing closer and closer together until they are today in fact more nearly united in understanding, in mutual trust, and even in organization for common action than ever before in Christian history. What has been taking place within the churches can on no account be put down as a phase of cultural drift. Rather, it discloses deep and powerful currents pressing resolutely and successfully directly against the most powerfully disruptive and centrifugal tides in contemporary culture

3. Third and last, ecumenical Christianity has been tested by fire, and thus far proved strong to endure. Today, this world Christian movement, youthful though it be, as yet embracing somewhat less than half of the eight hundred million Christians on the earth's surface and scarcely a sixth of the total populace of the world, tiny in organization, modest in pretention, does in fact hold in convinced allegiance representative leaders out of every race and almost every people, and binds them in a loyalty mightier than the most powerful parochialisms of nation or class. Moreover, it is a living, growing world community. It is the *only* true world community our earth knows. It may furnish to the despairing peoples of mankind an earnest, and something of a pattern, of the community of nations that someday may be.

NOTE

At the meeting of the Central Committee of the World Council of Churches at St. Andrews in August, 1960, a "Report of the Commission on Faith and Order on the Future of Faith and Order" was adopted, for transmission to the member churches for consideration and comment, which contained the following statement:

> The Committee on Faith and Order understands that the unity which is both God's will and his gift to his Church is one which brings all in each place[1] who confess Christ Jesus as Lord into a fully

[1] The word "place" here is used both in its primary sense of local neighborhood and also, under more modern conditions, of other areas in which Christians need to express unity in Christ, e.g., all those engaged in a local industry.

committed fellowship with one another through one baptism into him, holding the one apostolic faith, teaching the one gospel, breaking the one bread, and having a corporate life reaching out in witness and service to all; and which at the same time unites them with the whole Christian fellowship in all places and all ages in such wise that ministry and members are acknowledged by all and that all can act and speak together as occasion requires for the tasks to which God calls the Church.

At the St. Andrews meeting of the Central Committee, it was also voted to propose to the member churches at the Third Assembly in New Delhi in November, 1961, that the "Basis" of the World Council be altered from:

"The World Council of Churches is a fellowship of churches which accept our Lord Jesus Christ as God and Savior"

to read:

"The World Council of Churches is a fellowship of churches which confess the Lord Jesus Christ as God and Savior according to the Scriptures and therefore seek to fulfill together their common calling to the glory of the one God, Father, Son, and Holy Spirit."

Conclusion

CONCLUSION

We have summarized the accomplishments of Christianity in the period of which we are immediate heirs. We have appraised the promise which those accomplishments open for the church in the last half of the twentieth century. And we have sought to take the measure of the difficulties that must be met and mastered if that promise is to find fulfillment. If our forecast has seemed unduly apprehensive, it is because the circumstances of the time and the present state of Christendom would make any less sober outlook unrealistic. All that has been said adds up to this conclusion: the possibilities presented to Christians in our day are the most exciting and challenging ever faced by a single generation in the church's life, but they are shadowed by grave uncertainties. We may well make our own Paul's summary of his situation: "A wide door for effective work has opened to me, and there are many adversaries." It remains to draw from the record of the past certain guiding principles for the days ahead. Let me suggest four:

1. The first is to underscore the overarching lesson from recent history. The phenomenal achievements of "The Great Century" are the fruitage of not one but two mighty efforts among the Christian churches, each in fulfillment of an injunction attributed to the Lord of the church himself: to make disciples of all nations and to unite those disciples into one living community. And the two efforts belong together as complementary expressions of a single fidelity. "The connection between the movement for Christian reunion and the movement for world evangelization is of the deepest possible character. The two things are the two outward signs of a return to the heart of the gospel itself."[1] Ecumenical Christianity, after the figure of the body, is an organism functioning through two contrasted but inseparably interdependent arms. Neither can be rightly thought of without the other. Neither can function truly and effectively without the other.

[1] Newbigin, *op. cit.*, p. 19.

2. With respect to both aspects of the ecumenical movement, but especially the effort after Christian unity, there is no single and simple pathway forward. Advance must be pressed simultaneously along many alternative routes with equal vigor. The question is often put: Shall we seek Christian unity through organic church union, or through federation, or through co-operation in concrete tasks, or through deepening fellowship? As so often in human thought, a problem presented as a choice of either/or has its solution in the acceptance of both/and. Nothing stands forth from the record more clearly than the fact that the several types of church collaboration are not mutually exclusive alternatives between which choice must be made but complementary and mutually supporting routes toward a common goal. It is precisely the substantial advance along each of these several paths, and many more, that has made possible the epochal achievements in Christian unity in recent decades. There is every reason to expect that the same will hold true for further progress in the coming years.

Similarly, with respect to the Christian world mission, promise for its continuing progress lies not in work in any particular area or of any one type or under any single auspices. The glory of that mission today is to be discovered in the world Christian movement in its entirety, in its total sweep and reach, made up of thousands of individual centers sponsored by hundred of agencies in scores of lands on every continent. The largest hope for its future springs from the enlargement and intensification of all its multitudinous and multiform enterprises.

3. While the two movements are rightly viewed as correlative and advance in either has, on the whole, served the interests of the other also, the dynamic for both has, in the main, flowed from the effort for world evangelization. As we have said repeatedly, Christian missions have parented Christian unity. In an important sense, therefore, the former is prior and more important for the success of the total undertaking.

There is a corollary of this truth that deserves special attention. One of the most unexpected, and thus far neglected, conclusions from Professor Latourette's monumental surveys of the expansion of Christianity is this: In those periods of retreat that from time to time have overtaken the church and forced it back, losses have been most acute in those areas where Christian faith had been rooted longest and with greatest apparent security.

Time and again, these ancient centers of Christian strength
proved lacking in vitality adequate to withstand the disintegration of the cultures in which they had become enmeshed. As a
civilization crumbled, the churches linked to it faltered and often
fell. It was the relatively young and seemingly fragile churches
on the frontiers of civilization, not yet domesticated within their
enveloping culture, that proved strong to withstand the cata-
clysm and endured, shaken but unshattered. By the same token,
when retreat has given way to renewed advance, and the Christian movement has rallied for new outreach, vitality to requicken
the depleted organism has not come from the ancient centers;
they have been discovered inadequate to the task. On the contrary, power for fresh advance has come from those areas where
the church had been young when weakness set in, where its very
youth had enabled vigorous survival under attack, and where its
relative disengagement from the dying culture had fostered independence and creative life.[2]

The meaning of this unexpected fact for our day is clear. If
it should prove that "The Great Century" reached its climax with
the advent of the epoch of the "Great Wars," if we are entering
a period to be characterized by disintegration of culture and tem-
porary recession for the Christian cause, we know where we may
look for the centers of vitality that may be expected to empower
the advance that will surely someday be resumed. We should look
to the youngest Christian churches, but recently born of the
modern missionary outreach. In that perspective, the so-called
younger churches assume an importance all out of relation to
their size, maturity, and apparent strength.

4. Lastly, Christians may face the uncertainties ahead not only
with good hope born of their fundamental faith in the power of
God, but also with high confidence justified by what he has gra-
ciously accomplished through the weak and sinful organs of
Christ's church in these latter days. For the first time in its history, the church confronts both the promise and the perils of the
future as a world-wide reality, no longer limited to a single continent or area but firmly planted on every continent and in almost every nation, no longer so tied to a particular culture that it
would be imperiled by that culture's eclipse or collapse but
deeply rooted in peoples of every culture yet emancipated from

2 *The Unquenchable Light*, pp. 170 ff. Compare *World Christianity: Yesterday, Today, and Tomorrow*, pp. 64–65.

cultural servitude by their participation in a transcultural community. The world church enters that future as the bearer of a gospel whose ability to win the adherence of all men is no longer a hazard of faith but a proven fact established by the convinced allegiance of representative men and women of every class and type and race and culture of mankind. That God will in his own good time translate this anticipation of Christ's universal church into the actuality of that church in its fullness remains a cardinal article of faith. That he may utilize the coming decades to approximate that fulfillment should inspire the efforts of those who are privileged to guide the church to the eve of its third millennium, and cause them to lift up their eyes with eager expectation.

Appendixes

Appendixes

APPENDIX I

A CHRONOLOGY OF CHRISTIAN UNITY, 1795–1960

Prepared by the William Adams Brown Ecumenical Library,
Union Theological Seminary, New York

† Indicates events in connection with missions or younger churches.
§ Indicates interdenominational union of churches.
* Indicates union of churches.

†1795 London Missionary Society organized.

1796 New York Missionary Society founded.

1799 Religious Tract Society founded. London.

1801 Plan of Union between the Connecticut General Association (Congregational) and the General Assembly of the Presbyterian Church in the U.S.A. Terminated in 1837.

†1804 British and Foreign Bible Society organized.

†1810 American Board of Commissioners for Foreign Missions organized.

†1815 Basel Evangelical Missionary Society organized (Lutheran and Reformed).

1816 American Bible Society organized.

§1817 Prussian Evangelical Union, consisting of Lutheran and Calvinist congregations, constituted by direction of Frederick William III.

*1817 Synod of the Presbyterian Church of Nova Scotia organized by the Presbytery of Halifax, the Associate or Burgher Presbytery of Truro (1786), and the General Associate of Anti-Burgher Presbytery of Pictou (1795).

†1819 London Secretaries' Association initiated.

*1820 United Secession Church in Scotland formed by union of the main streams of Burghers, Anti-Burghers, and other Seceders having their origin in the schism of 1733 in the Church of Scotland and the organization of the Associate Presbytery.

1822 United Domestic Missionary Society founded.

†1822 Paris Evangelical Missionary Society organized.

1824 American Sunday School Union organized.

†1825 Bombay Missionary Union formed (Congregational Anglican, Presbyterian).

1825 American Tract Society organized.

Note: In most instances where an event is the first in a series recurring periodically or regularly only the initial event is recorded.

159

1826 American Home Missionary Society organized.

†1827 Madras Missionary Conference.

†1828 Rhenish Missionary Association formed (Lutheran and Reformed).

†1830 Calcutta Missionary Conference.

°1831 Presbyterian Church of Canada in Connection with the Church of Scotland organized by presbyteries in Lower Canada.

°1836 Wesleyan Methodist Association in England (organized in 1835 by a secession group from the Wesleyan Methodist Conference) enlarged by addition of the Protestant Methodists (organized in 1828).

†1837 Meeting of secretaries of four German Missionary Societies and the Paris Mission in Basel.

°1840 Presbyterian Church in Ireland formed by union of the Synod of Ulster and the Secession Synod of Ireland.

°1840 Synod of the Presbyterian Church of Canada in Connection with the Church of Scotland (1831) and the United Synod of Upper Canada (1831) united under the name of the former body.

†1841 Edinburgh Medical Missionary Society organized.

1844 Young Men's Christian Association founded in London.

†1846 American Missionary Association organized.

†1846 General Conference of German Missionary Societies.

1846 Evangelical Alliance organized in London.

°1847 United Presbyterian Church of Scotland formed by union of the United Secession Church (1820) and the Relief Church, a seceding body dating from 1761.

†1852 Zenana Bible and Medical Mission, an evangelical interdenominational society, founded for work in India.

†1854 Union Missionary Convention held in New York.

†1854 Anglo-Saxon Missionary Conference. London.

†1855 Netherlands Indies Missionary Union founded.

†1855 General Conference of Protestant missionaries in Bengal. Calcutta.

1855 World's Alliance of Young Men's Christian Associations organized at a conference held in Paris.

1855 Young Women's Christian Association founded in London.

†1857 North India Conference of Missionaries. Benares. North India and Ceylon.

°1857 United Methodist Free Churches formed in England by union of the Wesleyan Methodist Reformers and the Wesleyan Methodist Association.

†1858 Christian Literature Society for India founded (under the name Christian Vernacular Education Society).

†1858 South India Conference of Missionaries. Ootacamond.

*1858 United Presbyterian Church of North America formed by union of the Associate Reformed Presbyterian and the Associate Presbyterian Churches.

†1860 General conference on foreign missions. Liverpool.

*1860 Presbyterian Church of the Lower Provinces of British North America formed by union of the Presbyterian Church of Nova Scotia (1817) and the Free Church of Nova Scotia (originally organized in 1833 as the Synod of the Church of Scotland in Nova Scotia and Prince Edward Island).

†1860 Women's Union Missionary Society of America organized.

*1861 Canada Presbyterian Church formed by union of the Free Presbyterian Church of Canada (organized in 1844 by a secession group from the Synod of the Presbyterian Church in Canada in Connection with the Church of Scotland) and the United Presbyterian Church of Canada (first organized in 1834 as a missionary presbytery in the Canadas of the United Secession Church of Scotland).

1861 National Bible Society of Scotland organized.

†1862 Presbytery in Amoy formed (Presbyterian Church in England; Reformed Church in America).

†1862 Isan-Enim-Bolana Komity (federation of independent churches) established in Madagascar by London Missionary Society.

†1863 Hawaiian Evangelical Association organized.

†1863 Robert College, Istanbul, founded.

†1866 Continental Missions Conference. Bremen.

†1866 American University, Beirut, founded (under name of Syrian Protestant College).

*1866 Presbyterian Church of the Lower Provinces of British North America enlarged by addition of the Free Presbyterian Church of New Brunswick (a secession body organized in 1845).

1867 Lambeth Conference of bishops in communion with Church of England. First.

*1868 Synod of the Maritime Provinces in Connection with the Church of Scotland formed by union of the Synod of New Brunswick in Connection with the Church of Scotland (1833) and the Church of Scotland in Nova Scotia and Prince Edward Island (organized in 1854 by a secession group from the Synod of the Free Church of Nova Scotia).

*1869 Old and New School Presbyterians in the United States united, forming the Presbyterian Church in the United States of America.

†1869 Society of Friends joined with London Missionary Society in Isan-Enim-Bolana Komity in Madagascar.

†1872 Convention of Protestant missionaries in Japan. First. Yokohama.

†1872 Decennial missionary conference in India. First. Allahabad.

†1874 Mission to Lepers founded in England.

*1874 Methodist Church of Canada organized by the Conference of Wesleyan Methodists in the Canadas, the Conference of the Wesleyan Methodists in the Maritime Provinces, and the Canada Conference of the Methodist New Connection.

1875 Alliance of Reformed Churches Holding the Presbyterian System organized.

1875 International Sunday School Convention.

†1875 Istanbul Woman's College founded.

1875 Old Catholic unity conference. Bonn.

†1875 Presbyterian Alliance of India organized.

*1875 Presbyterian Church in Canada formed by union of the Presbyterian Church of Canada in Connection with the Church of Scotland (1840), the Presbyterian Church of the Lower Provinces of British North America (1860); Canada Presbyterian Church (1861), and the Synod of the Maritime Provinces in Connection with the Church of Scotland (1868).

†1876 Madras Christian College becomes a union institution (Baptist, Reformed, Presbyterian, Congregational, Methodist, Anglican).

*1876 Free Church of Scotland (organized as a result of the Disruption of 1843 in the Church of Scotland) enlarged by addition of the Reformed Presbyterian Church, a seceding body dating from 1743 (except a remnant not uniting).

†1876 India Sunday School Union organized.

*1876 Presbyterian Church of England formed by union of the English United Presbyterian Synod of the Presbyterian Church in England, and the Old English Presbyterian Churches.

*†1877 Church of Christ in Japan (Nihon Kirisuto Kyokwai) formed by union of churches connected with the missions of Presbyterian and Reformed Churches. First union on mission field.

†1877 General conference of Protestant missionaries of China. Shanghai.

†1878 General conference on foreign missions. London.

†1880 American Interseminary Missionary Alliance organized.

†1881 Ecumenical Methodist Conference. First meeting. London.

†1881 Natal Missionary Conference (Congregational, Presbyterian, Anglican, Holiness, Methodist, Lutheran). First.

†1884 International Missionary Union formed.

*1884 Methodist Church in Canada formed by union of the Primitive Methodist Church, the Bible Christian Church, the Methodist Episcopal Church, and the Methodist Church of Canada (1874).

†1884 Hislop College, Nagpur, founded (Presbyterian, Friends).

†1885 China Medical Missionary Association founded.

†1885 Standing Committee of German Missionary Societies formed.

†1886 Lingnan University, Canton, China, founded (under the name, Canton Christian College).

†1886 Student Volunteer Movement for Foreign Missions founded.

1886 Protestant Episcopal Church in the U.S.A. issued a Quadrilateral as a minimum basis for reunion of churches.

*†1887 Holy Catholic Church of Japan (Nihon Sei Ko Kwai) formed by union of churches connected with the missions of the Church of England and the Protestant Episcopal Church in the U.S.A.

1887 Christian Literature Society for China founded (under the name of Society for the Diffusion of Christian and General Knowledge).

†1888 Centenary conference of the Protestant missions of the world. London.

1888 Lambeth Conference. Third meeting. Adoption of the Lambeth Quadrilateral.

†1888 General Assembly of Evangelical Missionaries of Mexico. First. Mexico City.

*†1888 Presbyterian Church of Brazil formed by union of churches connected with the missions of the Presbyterian Church U.S.A. and the Presbyterian Church U.S.

1889 World's Sunday School Convention. First. London.

†1891 United Presbytery, Manchuria (United Presbyterian Church of Scotland and Presbyterian Church of Ireland).

†1891 Mission to the Aboriginals of North Queensland begun.

1891 International Congregational Council. First meeting. London.

†1893 Foreign Missions Conference of North America organized.

1894 World's Young Women's Christian Association organized.

†1895 French Reformed Church joined London Missionary Society and Friends in Isan-Enim-Bolana Komity in Madagascar (sometimes called Malagasy Protestant Church).

1895 World's Christian Endeavor Union organized.

1895 World's Student Christian Federation founded at Vadstena, Sweden.

1896 National Council of the Evangelical Free Churches in England organized.

*1896 United Evangelical Lutheran Church (designated the United Danish Evangelical Lutheran Church until 1945) formed by merger of the Danish Church Association and the Danish Church in North America.

†1897 Committee of General Reference established by Foreign Missions Conference of North America.

†1897 South India Missionary Association formed.

*1897 Presbyterian Church of South Africa formed by union of English-speaking churches of Presbyterian faith and polity in South Africa.

†1899 West China Missionary Conference. West China Advisory Board of Missions founded.

†1900 Ecumenical conference on foreign missions. New York.

†1900 United Missionary Conference, Nyasaland.

*1900 United Free Church of Scotland formed by union of the United Presbyterian Church of Scotland (1847) and the Free Church of Scotland (except a fragment not uniting).

†1901 Evangelical Union of the Philippines organized (becomes National Christian Council in 1929).

*†1901 South India United Church (Presbyterian Synod) formed by merger of churches connected with the missions of the United Free Church of Scotland and the Reformed Church in America. First stage in the development of the South India United Church.

*1901 Presbyterian Church of Australia organized.

*1901 Presbyterian Church of New Zealand formed by union of the Presbyterian churches in north and south New Zealand.

†1902 Congo Missionary Conference inaugurated.

†1902 Federation of Christian Missions in Japan organized.

†1902 Missionary Education Movement of the United States and Canada organized.

†1903 North China Educational Union formed.

†1903 Southern Rhodesia Missionary Conference (Anglican, Congregational, Brethren, Reformed, Methodist, Presbyterian, Church of Christ). First.

†1904 Shantung Christian University founded (Baptist and Northern Presbyterian).

†1904 General Missionary Conference of South Africa organized. Johannesburg.

*1904 Methodist Church of Australasia organized.

*†1904 Presbyterian Church of India formed by merger of seven Presbyterian bodies.

1905 Baptist World Alliance. First meeting. London.

†1905 Transvaal Missionary Association founded.

*†1905 Congregational General Union in South India formed by union of churches connected with the missions of the Congregational Churches of England and the United States.

†1905 Federation of Evangelical Churches of Puerto Rico formed.

†1905 National Missionary Society of India founded.

†1905 General Council of Evangelical Missions, Korea, founded.

1905 International Sunday School Association succeeded the International Sunday School Convention (1875).

†1906 Zendings Consulaat (Indonesia) organized.

†1906 American Mission to Lepers organized.

†1906 Educational Union of West China founded.

†1906 Union Christian College, Pyengyang, Korea, founded.

†1906 Union Medical College, Peking, founded.

†1906 Laymen's Missionary Movement founded in the United States.

†1906 Missionary conference on behalf of Christian work in the Mohammedan world. First. Cairo.

*1907 Congregational Union of Canada formed by union of the Congregational Union of Nova Scotia and New Brunswick, the Congregational Union of Ontario and Quebec, and the Ontario Conference of the United Brethren in Christ.

*†1907 Japan Methodist Church formed by union of churches connected with the missions of the Methodist Church in Canada, the Methodist Episcopal Church, and the Methodist Episcopal Church, South, in the United States.

*†1907 Presbyterian Church in Korea formed by union of churches connected with the missions of the Presbyterian Church in Canada, the Presbyterian Church of Australia, the Presbyterian Church U.S.A., and the Presbyterian Church U.S.

†1907 Union Theological Seminary founded in Manila (Anglican, Methodist, Presbyterian, Disciple).

†1907 Union Theological Seminary, Indore, Central India, founded by Malwa Church Council (Northern India) in co-operation with Canadian missionaries. Scotch Presbyterian mission joined in 1933.

*1907 United Methodist Church formed in England by union of the United Methodist Free Churches (1857), the Methodist New Connection, and the Bible Christian Church.

1907 World's Sunday School Association organized.

†1908 Transkeian (South Africa) Missionary Conference (Anglican, Methodist, Moravian, Presbyterian, Reformed).

†1908 All-India Lutheran Conference organized.

1908 Council of Women for Home Missions in the United States organized.

1908 Federal Council of the Churches of Christ in America organized.

1908 Home Missions Council in the United States organized.

†1908 North China Union Medical College for Women, Peking, organized.

†1908 East African General Conference. First. Nairobi, Kenya.

§†1908 South India United Church formed by merger of the Congregational General Union in South India and the South India United Church (Presbyterian Synod).

1909 French Protestant Federation organized.

†1909 University of Shanghai founded, with co-operation of the Northern Baptist Convention and the Southern Baptist Convention in the United States.

†1910 Hangchow Christian College, Hangchow, China, became a union institution.

†1910 Union Medical College, Tsinan, founded.

†1910 Kwansei Gakuin, Nishinomiya, Japan, organized as a union institution.

†1910 Federated Missions, Japan, formed (made up of a group of missionaries).

†1910 Serampore College, India, Theological Department, opened as a union school (Congregational, Baptist, Methodist, Presbyterian, Lutheran).

†1910 Union Theological College, Madagascar, founded (Congregational, Friends).

†1910 United Theological College at Banglore, India, founded (Congregational, Reformed, Methodist, South India United Church).

†1910 National Convention of Baptists. Mexico.

†1910 University of Nanking (including the university hospital) formed by merger of educational and medical institutions in Nanking (Baptist, Methodist, Presbyterian, Disciple).

†1910 West China Union University founded at Chengtu (Baptist, Methodist, Anglican, Friends).

†1910 World Missionary Conference. Edinburgh.

 1910 Sunday School Council of evangelical denominations formed.

†1911 Federal Council of Protestant Evangelical Missions in Korea formed (succeeds General Council of Evangelical Missions in Korea, 1905).

†1911 Federation of Churches, Japan.

†1911 Nanking Theological Seminary organized as a union institution through the merger of three denominational schools in Nanking (Methodist, Presbyterian, Disciple).

†1912 Christian Literature Society of Japan organized.

†1912 Conference of Missionary Societies in Great Britain and Ireland organized.

†1912 Moukden Medical College organized (Presbyterian and Lutheran).

†1912 Danish Missions Council organized.

°†1912 Holy Catholic Church in China (Chung Hua Sheng Kung Hui) organized by union of churches connected with the missions of the Church of England, the Church of England in Canada, and the Protestant Episcopal Church in the United States of America.

†1912 Bible Teachers' Training School, Nanking, is made union enterprise (Methodist, Presbyterian, Disciple).

†1912 Union Mission Tuberculosis Sanatorium, Arogyavaram, India, founded.

†1913 Intermissionary Committee of Madagascar organized.

†1913 Committee on Co-operation in Latin America organized.

†1913 Central China Union Theological Seminary, Wuchang, organized (Methodist, Presbyterian, Reformed, Evangelical, Congregational).

†1913 Union Bible Seminary, Chile, founded (Methodist, Presbyterian).

†1913 National Missionary Council of India, Burma, and Ceylon organized. Also eight (later ten) Provincial Councils.

†1913 Severence Union Medical College, Seoul, Korea, organized as a union institution.

1914 Church Peace Union founded.

1914 Fellowship of Reconciliation founded.

1914 General Missionary Conference, Northern Rhodesia. First. Present: Primitive Methodist, Brethren in Christ, Paris Evangelical Mission, Wesleyan Methodist, Universities Mission to Central Africa (Anglican). At the third meeting in 1922, in addition to the above, the following were represented: Livingstonia Mission (United Free Church of Scotland) Baptist, Adventists, London Missionary Society, Dutch Reformed, and Roman Catholic (Jesuit).

†1914 Union Bible Women's Training School, Peking, founded (Congregational, Presbyterian, Methodist).

†1914 Union Theological College, Canton, China, organized (Church Missionary Society, Brethren, Presbyterian, Congregational, Methodist).

†1914 Pierson Memorial Bible School, Seoul, founded (Methodist, Presbyterian).

1914 World Alliance for International Friendship Through the Churches founded.

†1915 Chosen Christian College, Seoul, Korea, founded as a union institution (Methodist, Presbyterian).

†1915 Ginling College, Nanking, founded as a union institution (Congregational, Disciple, Baptist, Presbyterian, Reformed, Methodist, Protestant Episcopal).

†1915 Aoyama Gakuin, Theological Department, established as a union project (Methodist, Evangelical, Disciple).

†1915 Women's Christian College, Madras, founded as a union institution (Congregational, Presbyterian, Lutheran, Reformed, Anglican, Methodist, Baptist).

†1916 Evangelical Union of Puerto Rico organized as successor to the Federation of Evangelical Churches (1905).

†1916 Regional Conferences held in South America in Peru, Chile,

Argentina, Brazil, Colombia, Cuba, Puerto Rico.

†1916 Panama Congress on Christian Work in Latin America.

†1916 Federation of Woman's Boards of Foreign Missions of North America organized.

†1916 Fukien Christian University, Foochow, China, organized as a union institution (Congregational, Methodist, Reformed, Anglican).

†1916 Committee on Co-operation in Brazil organized.

 1916 South African Native College, Fort Hare, established through co-operation of churches and government.

†1916 Yenching University, Peiping, organized as a union institution (Congregational, Methodist, Presbyterian).

†1917 Cheeloo University, Tsinan, China (including a theological school, a medical school and hospital), formed by merger of educational and medical institutions, called Shantung Christian University until 1931 (Baptist, Congregational, Presbyterian, Lutheran, Methodist, Anglican).

†1917 Committee on Co-operation in Mexico organized.

†1917 Union Evangelical Seminary, Mexico, founded (Congregational, Friends, Methodist, Disciple).

*1917 Evangelical Lutheran Church (designated the Norwegian Lutheran Church of America until 1946) formed by union of the Norwegian Synod, the United Norwegian Lutheran Church, and Hauge's Synod.

†1918 Finnish Mission Council organized.

*†1918 Presbyterian Churches in China unite.

†1918 Fourah Bay College, Freetown, Sierra Leone, becomes a union institution (Anglican, Methodist).

†1918 Alliance of Missionary Societies in British East Africa (Kenya) organized (Congregational, Presbyterian, Methodist, Africa Inland Mission).

†1918 Isabella Thoburn College, Lucknow, becomes a union institution (Presbyterian, Methodist).

†1918 Vellore Medical College for Women, Vellore, India, opened.

†1918 Union Theological Seminary, Gooty, South India, organized (Reformed, Congregational).

†1918 Woman's Christian College of Japan, Tokyo, founded as a union institution (Presbyterian, Reformed, Disciple, Baptist, Methodist).

 1918 National Lutheran Council in the United States organized.

*1918 United Lutheran Church in America formed by union of the General Synod of the Evangelical Lutheran Church in the United States of America, the General Council of the Evangelical Lutheran Church in North America, and the United Synod of the Evangelical Lutheran Church in the South.

†1918 Federal Council of Churches, Korea, founded (Presbyterian, Methodist).

†1919 Evangelical Theological Seminary of Puerto Rico founded at Rio Piedras (Baptist, Congregational, Methodist, Presbyterian, Brethren, Disciple).

†1919 Margaret Williamson Hospital, Shanghai, organized as a union institution.

†1919 Negotiations opened for the formation of an all-inclusive united church in South India.

*†1919 Tamil Evangelical Lutheran Church formed by union of churches developed by the Leipzig Evangelical Lutheran Mission and the Church of Sweden Mission in India.

†1919 Union Theological Seminary, Buenos Aires, becomes a union institution (Methodist, Disciple, Presbyterian).

†1919 United Missionary Council of Syria and Palestine formed.

1919 Federal Council of the Evangelical Free Churches in England organized.

1919 United Theological Seminary in Madrid founded.

†1920 American University at Cairo opened.

†1920 Board of Christian Work in Santo Domingo organized, with headquarters in New York.

†1920 Kinnaird College, Lahore, organized as a union institution (Presbyterian, United Presbyterian, Anglican, Zenana).

*†1920 Lutheran Church of China formed by churches connected with the missions established by Lutheran bodies in Europe and America.

†1920 Swedish Mission Council organized.

1920 Swiss Protestant Federation organized.

†1920 United Missionary Council of Australia organized.

1920 Universal Christian Conference on the Life and Work of the Church of Christ. Preliminary meeting. Geneva.

*1920 Welsh Calvinistic Methodist Churches in the United States united with the Presbyterian Church in the United States of America.

1920 World Conference on Faith and Order. Preliminary meeting. Geneva.

†1921 International Missionary Council organized, in succession to the Continuation Committee appointed at Edinburgh in 1910.

1921 New Zealand Council of Religious Education organized through co-operation of six denominations.

†1921 Silliman Bible School, Philippines, founded (Congregational, Presbyterian).

†1921 Norwegian Mission Council organized.

†1922 Angola Evangelical Missions Conference. Evangelical Alliance of Angola founded.

1922 Central Bureau for European Interchurch Aid organized.

*1922 Evangelical Church formed in the United States by union of the Evangelical Association and the United Evangelical Church.

1922 German Evangelical Church Federation organized.

1922 International conference of church leaders at Copenhagen to consider relief for Protestant Europe.

†1922 German Evangelical Missions Federation organized.

†1922 National Christian Council of China organized.

†1922 National Christian Council of India, Burma, and Ceylon organized as successor to the National Missionary Council (1913). Also ten Provincial Councils organized.

1922 International Council of Religious Education (designated the International Sunday School Council of Religious Education until 1925) formed by merger of the International Sunday School Association (1905) and the Sunday School Council of Evangelical Churches (1910).

†1923 Association of Swiss Missions for International Relations organized.

†1923 Woodstock Teachers' Training College (India) becomes union enterprise (Presbyterian and United Presbyterian). Six other groups joined in 1927 (Baptist, Methodist, United Church of Canada, Brethren, Young Men's Christian Association, United Christian Missionary Society).

1923 Lutheran World Convention. First meeting. Eisenach, Germany.

†1923 National Christian Council of Japan organized.

†1923 Northern Missionary Council organized with representatives from Denmark, Finland, Norway, and Sweden.

†1923 St. Christopher's Training College, Madras, founded as a union institution.

1923 Federation of the Evangelical Churches of Spain formed.

*†1924 Church of Central Africa, Presbyterian, formed by union of churches connected with the mission work of the Church of Scotland, and the United Free Church of Scotland.

1924 Conference on Christian Politics, Economics, and Citizenship. Birmingham, England.

†1924 Conference of Christian Workers among Moslems. Jerusalem.

†1924 Forman Christian College (founded in 1886), Lahore, becomes a union institution (Methodist, Presbyterian).

†1924 Hua Chung College, Wuchang, formed by merger of five denominational institutions in central China (Reformed, Protestant Episcopal, Congregational, Methodist).

†1924 Kenya Missionary Council organized (Anglican, Friends, Church of God, Presbyterian, Methodist, Reformed, Adventist).

†1924 Korean National Christian Council organized.

†1924 United Christian Council organized in Sierra Leone.

§†1924 United Church of Northern India formed by union of the Congregational Churches in Western India and the Presbyterian Church of India (1904).

†1924 United Mission in Mesopotamia established as a joint enterprise of the Presbyterian Church U.S.A., the Reformed Church in America, and the Reformed Church in the United States.

†1924 Woman's Christian Medical College, Shanghai, organized as a union institution.

†1925 Intermission Council of the Northern Sudan organized.

†1925 Congo Protestant Council organized.

†1925 All-Persia Interchurch Conference. Hamadan.

†1925 Congress on Christian Work in South America. Montevideo.

†1925 Ewha College, Seoul, Korea, became a union institution (Methodist, United Church of Canada).

†1925 Ciskeian (South Africa) Missionary Council organized (Methodist, Presbyterian, Baptist, Anglican, Ethiopian, Congregational, Reformed, Moravian).

*1925 Evangelical Protestant churches of North America merged with the Congregational churches.

§1925 United Church of Canada formed by union of the Methodist Church (1884), the Congregational Union (1907), and the Presbyterian Church (1875) except a part not uniting.

1925 Universal Christian Conference on Life and Work. Stockholm.

†1926 Federation of Evangelical Lutheran Churches in India organized, as successor to the All-India Lutheran Conference (1908).

*†1926 Presbyterian Church of the Gold Coast formed by union of churches connected with missions of the Church of Scotland and the Basel Missionary Society.

†1926 Northern India United Theological College, Saharanpur, became union institution (Presbyterian, Anglican, Baptist).

†1926 Persia Council organized.

†1926 Swiss Committee of Missions organized.

†1926 Conference on "The Christian Mission in Africa." Le Zoute, Belgium.

*†1926 Church of Central Africa enlarged by Dutch Reformed Presbytery of Mkhoma.

§†1927 Church of Christ in China organized (Presbyterian, Congregational, English Baptist, Methodist, Reformed, United Brethren, United Church of Canada).

†1927 National Missionary Council of Australia organized.

†1927 National Missionary Council of New Zealand organized.

†1927 Interchurch Conference of Persia organized.

†1927 Near East Christian Council organized (under the name of Christian Council for Western Asia and Northern Africa).

†1927 Near East College Association organized, with headquarters in New York.

1927 World Conference on Faith and Order. Lausanne.

†1927 Doshisha University, Japan, theological department becomes a union enterprise (Congregational, United Brethren).

†1928 Shung Kei Bible Training School, Kwantung, began as union institution (Presbyterian, Brethren, Congregational, Methodist).

†1928 International Missionary Council, World Conference at Jerusalem.

†1928 National Evangelical Council in Mexico organized.

†1928 Wanless Tuberculosis Sanatorium opened at Miraj, India (Presbyterian, Congregational).

†1929 Christian Council of Nigeria organized.

†1929 Christian Council of the Gold Coast organized.

†1929 Near East Christian Council organized under this name (see 1927).

†1929 Hispanic American Evangelical Congress at Havana.

†1929 Lady Irwin Tuberculosis Sanatorium, Simla Hills, India, founded as a union project.

*1929 Church of Scotland formed by merger of the Church of Scotland and the United Free Church of Scotland (except a fragment not uniting).

1929 International Committee on Christian Literature for Africa formed under the auspices of the International Missionary Council.

†1929 National Christian Council of the Philippines organized as successor to the Evangelical Union (1901) (see 1938).

†1929 Netherlands Mission Council organized.

†1929 Union Theological College, Foochow, China, organized as a union institution.

†1929 First Round Table Conference, North India (Methodist, United Church of Northern India).

†1929 Newman School of Missions, Palestine, organized.

§†1929 United Evangelical Church of the Philippines formed by merger of the United Brethren, Congregational, and Presbyterian Churches.

†1929 National Christian Council of Siam formed.

*1930 American Lutheran Church formed by union of the Evangelical Lutheran Synod of Ohio and Other States, the Evangelical Lutheran Synod of Iowa and Other States, and the Lutheran Synod of Buffalo.

1930 Universal Christian Council on Life and Work formed.

1930 American Lutheran Conference organized as a federation for co-operative action. Members: American Lutheran Church; Evangelical Lutheran Augustana Synod of North America; Evangelical Lutheran Church (then the Norwegian Lutheran Church of America); Lutheran Free Church; United Evangelical Lutheran Church in America (then the United Danish Evangelical Lutheran Church in America).

†1930 Henry Martyn School of Islamics opened at Lahore (in 1941 moved to Aligarh).

*†1930 Korean Methodist Church formed by union of the Methodist Episcopal and Methodist Episcopal, South, Churches.

†1930 United Theological College of Western India, Poona, founded (Congregational, Methodist, Presbyterian, United Church of Northern India).

*†1930 Methodist Church of Mexico formed by union of the Methodist Episcopal and Methodist Episcopal, South, Churches.

1930 North American Home Missions Congress, Washington.

†1930 Wilson College, Bombay, founded by the Church of Scotland, becomes a union institution (Congregational, Presbyterian).

1930 World Convention of the Churches of Christ (Disciples). First meeting. Washington.

†1931 Federation of Evangelical Churches, Brazil. Became Evangelical Confederation of Brazil in 1934.

*†1931 Ewe Presbyterian Church in West Africa organized by churches connected with the Paris Evangelical Missionary Society, the Church of Scotland, and the former work of the Bremen Mission.

*1931 Methodist Church of South Africa formed by union of the Wesleyan Methodist Church of South Africa, the Transvaal and Swaziland District of the Wesleyan Methodist Church in England, and the Primitive Methodist missions in the Union of South Africa.

†1931 National Committee for Christian Religious Education organized in China.

†1931 All-India Conference on Church Union. Nagpur.

§†1931 United Evangelical Church in Puerto Rico formed by union of the United Brethren, Christian, and Congregational Churches.

§1931 Congregational-Christian Churches organized in the United States by merger of the Congregational and Christian churches.

†1932 Associated Boards for Christian Colleges in China organized, with headquarters in New York.

*1932 Methodist Church in England formed by union of the Wesleyan Methodists, the Primitive Methodist Church, and the United Methodist Church (1907).

1932 Lovedale Bible School, South Africa, founded (Presbyterian,

Anglican, Congregational, Methodist, Baptist).

†1932 Near East School of Theology formed by merger of the School of Religion, Athens, and the School for Religious Workers, Beirut.

†1933 German Evangelical Missionary Conference took the place of the German Evangelical Missions Federation.

†1933 Inter-Mission Council of the Northern Sudan reconstituted.

†1933 United Missionary Training College, Bengal, formed as union institution combining two smaller schools (Baptist, Anglican, Presbyterian, Congregational).

†1933 Scheme of union adopted by Union Committee of the Inter-church Conference of Persia (see 1934).

†1934 Association of Evangelical Churches of Puerto Rico succeeded the Evangelical Union (1916).

†1934 Anglicans, Methodists, and Presbyterians in South Africa issue Scheme of Union.

§†1934 Church of Christ in Siam formed by union of the Presbyterian and Baptist churches.

§†1934 Evangelical and Reformed Church constituted by union of the Evangelical Synod of North America and the Reformed Church in the United States.

†1934 Evangelical Confederation of Brazil organized.

1934 United Christian Youth Movement organized in North America.

†1935 United Society for Christian Literature formed in England by merger of the Religious Tract Society (1799) and the Christian Literature Society for India and Africa (1858).

†1935 All-Japan Christian Conference approves basis of church union. Commission on Church Union appointed.

†1935 Church Unity Conference. Shanghai.

1936 Christian Council of South Africa organized.

1936 Congregationalists, Methodists, and Presbyterians in South Africa issue "Preliminary Basis of Union."

*†1936 Evangelical Church in Guatemala formed by union of the Presbyterian Churches and the Central American Mission.

†1936 Union Theological Seminary, Pasumalai, South India, becomes a union institution (Presbyterian, Congregational, South India United Church).

§†1936 United Missions in the Copper Belt in Northern Rhodesia established. By-product of this is Union Church of the Copper Belt (Congregational, Presbyterian, Methodist).

1937 Interseminary Movement, as successor to the American Inter-seminary Missionary Alliance (1880), organized under the auspices of the American Committee for the World Council of Churches and the Young Men's Christian Association.

†1937 West China Union Theological College founded at Chengtu, China.

1937 World Conference on Church, Community, and State, sponsored by the Universal Christian Council for Life and Work. Oxford.

1937 World Conference on Faith and Order. Edinburgh.

1937 Protestant Episcopal Church, General Convention, issues an invitation to the Presbyterian Church U.S.A., to enter into negotiations to achieve organic union.

†1938 Philippine Federation of Evangelical Churches replaces the National Christian Council formed in 1929.

§†1938 United Church of Northern India enlarged by accession of the churches connected with the mission of the Evangelical and Reformed Church.

1938 Presbyterian Church U.S.A., General Assembly, accepted the proposal of the Protestant Episcopal Church to open negotiations on church union.

§1938 Reformed Church of France formed by union of the Free Evangelical Churches, The Methodist Church, the Reformed Evangelical Church, and the Reformed Church.

1938 Utrecht Conference of representatives of the churches, convened by the Committee of Fourteen, to prepare a draft constitution for a proposed world council of churches.

†1938 International Missionary Council. World Conference. Madras.

†1939 Confederation of Evangelical Churches of the River Plate organized.

1939 Ecumenical Refugee Commission of the World Council of Churches organized.

†1939 First Evangelical Congress of Mexico (participated in by Baptist, Congregationalist, Disciple, Episcopalian, Nazarene, and Presbyterian delegates).

*1939 The Methodist Church (U.S.A.) formed by union of the Methodist Episcopal Church; the Methodist Episcopal Church, South; and the Methodist Protestant Church.

1939 Presbyterian Church U.S.A., and Presbyterian Church U.S., Joint Committee on Union, issues proposed "basic principles for union."

†1939 Near East Christian Council reorganized on an ecclesiastical basis.

†1939 "Basis of Negotiation," North India, issued (Baptist, Anglican, Methodist, United Church of Northern India).

†1939 Willis F. Pierce Memorial Hospital established at Foochow, China, through union of medical institutions of the Congregational and Methodist Churches.

1939 World Council of Churches, Provisional Committee meeting. Paris.

1939 World Conference of Christian Youth. Amsterdam.

1940 Church union negotiations begun in New Zealand by the Congregational, Methodist, and Presbyterian Churches.

†1940 Fifth meeting of Joint Council (Baptist, Methodist, United Church of Northern India) issues Plan of Union, North India.

1940 Federal Council of the Churches of Christ in America authorizes the formation of a Commission on a Just and Durable Peace.

1940 Free Church Federal Council formed in England by merger of the Federal Council of the Evangelical Free Churches (1919) and the National Council of the Evangelical Free Churches (1896.)

1940 Home Missions Council of North America formed by merger of the Home Missions Council (1908) and the Council of Women for Home Missions (1908).

1940 Australian Intercommunion Group (unofficial) of Anglicans, Congregationalists, Methodists, and Presbyterians issues a proposal for the "interchange of ministerial commissions."

†1940 Latin-American Student Christian Movement organized.

1940 Northern Ecumenical Insitute ("Ecumenicum") established at Sigtuna, Sweden.

†1941 Christian Council of Jamaica organized.

*†1941 Church of Christ in Japan (Nihon Kirusuto Kyodan) organized (Anglican, Baptist, Congregational, Disciple, Evangelical and Reformed, Evangelical United Brethren, Lutheran, Methodist, Presbyterian, Reformed, Church of Canada), 41 bodies.

†1941 Council of Evangelical Churches in Cuba organized.

1941 International Congress on Christian Education, Mexico City, under the auspices of the National Council of Evangelical Churches of Mexico and the World's Sunday School Association, North America Committee.

1941 Latin American Evangelical Youth Conference. First. Lima, Peru.

*†1941 Methodist Church in China formed by union of churches connected with the former Methodist Episcopal Church, Methodist Episcopal Church, South, and Methodist Protestant Church in the United States.

†1941 Methodist Church in South India accepts the Proposed Scheme of Church Union in South India.

1941 National Council of Churches in New Zealand organized.

†1941 National Evangelical Council of Peru organized.

1941 North American Ecumenical Conference held in Toronto, with representatives present from Latin America, United States, and Canada.

1941 United Council of Church Women organized in the United States.

1942 British Council of Churches organized.

1942 Committees on Christian unity of the Congregational, Methodist, and Presbyterian Churches in Australia adopted proposals on church union to be submitted to the three denominational bodies.

1942 Evangelical and Reformed Church and the Congregational Christian Churches in the United States initiate negotiations to achieve organic union.

†1942 Christian Council of Nyasaland organized.

†1943 Christian Council of Kenya organized.

†1943 United Theological Seminary at Kerala, South India, opened.

1944 Canadian Council of Churches organized.

†1944 Christian Council of Mozambique organized.

†1944 Christian Council of Northern Rhodesia organized.

1944 Reformed Church in America and the United Presbyterian Church of North America initiated negotiations to achieve organic union.

†1944 Swiss Council of Missions formed by merger of the Swiss Missions Committee (1926) and the Association of Swiss Missions for International Relations (1923).

1944 United Student Christian Council organized in the United States.

†1945 Church of India, Burma, and Ceylon, General Council, vote permission to four dioceses in South India to enter into union with the Methodist and South India United Churches, as provided in the Proposed Scheme of Church Union.

§†1945 Church of Central Africa in Rhodesia formed by union of the Congregational Churches connected with the London Missionary Society, the Union Church of the Copper Belt, and the Church of Central Africa (Presbyterian).

1945 Council of Protestant Churches in Poland organized.

†1945 United Andean Indian Mission organized, in which the Evangelical and Reformed Church, Presbyterian Church U.S., Presbyterian Church U.S.A., and the Church of the United Brethren in Christ co-operate.

§†1945 United Church of Northern India enlarged by accession of the Congregational Churches in Bengal connected with the London Missionary Society.

†1946 Church union negotiating committee in Ceylon, representing the Baptist Church, the Church of India, Burma, and Ceylon, The Methodist Church, the Presbyterian Church, and the Jaffna Council of the South India United Church, issue a basis of union for the consideration of the churches.

1946 Australian section of the World Council of Churches organized.

1946 Church of England in Canada and the United Church of Canada report for study in the churches a plan for a mutually acceptable ministry.

†1946 The South India United Church accepts the Proposed Scheme

of Church Union with the Church of India, Burma, and Ceylon and The Methodist Church to form the Church of South India.

†1946 Church World Service formed in the United States by merger of the Church Committee on Overseas Relief and Reconstruction, the Commission for World Council Service, and the Church Committee for Relief in Asia.

1946 Commission of the Churches on International Affairs organized under the auspices of the World Council of Churches and the International Missionary Council.

1946 Ecumenical Council of the Churches in Holland organized.

†1946 Evangelical Theological Seminary opened at Matanzas, Cuba.

†1946 International Missionary Council, Ad Interim Committee meeting. Geneva.

†1946 Korea National Christian Council re-established.

†1946 Peruvian Evangelical Church. First general assembly.

§1946 Evangelical United Brethren Church formed in the United States by union of Evangelical Church (1922) and the Church of the United Brethren in Christ.

1946 Federal Council of the Evangelical Churches in Italy organized.

†1946 Reformed Church in America begins co-operation with the United Presbyterian Church in Christian work in the South Sudan.

1946 United Bible Societies organized.

*1946 United Methodist Church in Italy formed by union of the Methodist Episcopal Church of Italy and the Wesleyan Methodist Church of Italy.

†1946 United Youth Conference of the Western Hemisphere, sponsored by the Latin American Union of Evangelical Youth, the United Christian Youth Movement in the United States, and the World's Sunday School Association. Havana.

†1946 West Central Africa Christian Conference. Leopoldville, Belgian Congo.

§†1946 Decision to continue Kyodan (Church of Christ in Japan) (Northern Baptist, Congregational, Disciple, Evangelical and Reformed, Evangelical United Brethren, Methodist, Presbyterian, Reformed, Church of Canada).

*1946 The Dutch Reformed Church and the Reformed Churches in the Netherlands (in Restored Connection) unite to form the Dutch Reformed Church.

†1947 Allahabad Agricultural Institute in India (first opened in 1911) becomes a union institution.

†1947 Ceylon National Christian Council formed by separation from the National Christian Council of India, Burma, and Ceylon.

§†1947 Church of South India organized by merger of the South India United Church, Methodist Church (Provincial Synod of South

India), and four dioceses of the Church of India, Burma, and Ceylon.

†1947 Japan Sunday School Association. In 1948 becomes the Japan Council of Christian Education.

†1947 Korea Sunday School Association (dissolved in 1938 by Japanese orders) re-established. In 1948 becomes the Korea Council of Christian Education.

1947 Lutheran World Federation organized as successor to the Lutheran World Convention.

1947 National Council of Churches of Czechoslovakia organized.

†1947 Philippine Federation of Christian Churches formed by merger of the Philippine Federation of Evangelical Churches (1938) and the Philippine Committee on Christian Education.

1947 World Conference of Christian Youth. Oslo.

1947 World Council of Christian Education organized as successor to the World's Sunday School Association (1907).

†1947 Meeting of the International Missionary Council. Whitby, Canada.

†1948 Conversations on church union opened by Baptists, Lutherans, and the Church of South India.

1948 Council of Christian Publishers in China supersedes the United Christian Publishers.

1948 World Council of Churches. First Assembly. Amsterdam.

†1948 Council of Co-operation for Christian Work in Japan formed for official relations with mission boards in the West.

†1948 Japan International Christian University foundation organized.

†1948 Joint Commission on Eastern Asia formed by the International Missionary Council and the World Council of Churches.

*1948 Evangelical Church in Germany formed from twenty-seven independent regional Churches.

†1948 Korea Inter-Mission Co-operative Committee organized.

†1948 Malaya Christian Council organized.

†1948 National Christian Council of Japan reconstituted.

†1948 Okinawa Christian Association, a nondenominational indigenous body, formed.

†1948 Union Theological College, Singapore (renamed Trinity College) established by Methodists, Presbyterians, and Anglicans.

§†1948 United Church of Christ in the Philippines organized by merger of the Evangelical Church in the Philippines, Philippine Methodist Church, and the United Evangelical Church (Presbyterian, Congregational, Evangelical United Brethren, Disciple, Methodist).

†1949 Burma Christian Council formed by separation from the National Christian Council of India and Burma.

†1949 East Asian Christian Conference under the auspices of the International Missionary Council and the World Council of Churches. Bangkok, Thailand.

†1949 Latin America Evangelical Conference. Buenos Aires.

†1949 Leonard Theological College, Jubbulpore, India, becomes a union institution (Methodist, five others).

*†1949 Presbyterian Church of the New Hebrides formed by churches connected with Presbyterian missions from Canada, Australia, and New Zealand.

†1949 School of Theology, Rhodes University, South Africa, supported by Congregational, Anglican, Baptist, Methodist, Presbyterian, Churches of Christ.

†1950 National Council of Churches in Indonesia formed at Djakarta with delegates from twenty-one of Indonesia's twenty-nine churches.

†1950 Christian Council of West Pakistan formed from the Christian Council of India and Pakistan at Nagpur.

*†1950 Tamil Lutheran Church Synod formed (Tamil Evangelical Lutheran Church Council and Church of Sweden Missionary Council).

*†1950 Cleavage in Syrian Orthodox Church of India healed by a round-table agreement among the eleven bishops of the church at Chingavanam, Travancore, India.

*1950 Evangelical Free Church of America formed from two bodies.

1950 Christian unity meeting of leaders of the Anglican, Roman Catholic, and Free Churches held at Canterbury, England.

*†1950 Federation of four Evangelical Churches of German origin in Brazil.

1950 German Evangelical Assembly (Kirchentag). First. Essen.

1950 Constituting Convention of the National Council of the Churches of Christ in the United States of America at Cleveland.

*†1950 Madagasy Lutheran Church formed by union.

1950 Annual Conference of The Methodist Church in New Zealand votes to support union with the Presbyterian and Congregational Churches. The Presbyterian General Assembly in New Zealand instructs its committee to meet representatives of co-operating churches to formulate a common policy in union matters.

†1951 United Church of Northern India adds the words "and Pakistan" to its name.

*†1951 Presbyterian Church in Formosa formed from the union of the Presbyterian Church of South Formosa and the Church in North Formosa.

†1951 North Celebes Regional Council of five churches begins.

†1951 Indonesian Council of Chinese Churches with eleven denominations begins.

†1951 Conference on Arab Refugee problems. Jointly convened by I. M. C. and W. C. C. Beirut.

†1951 Tamilnad Theological College, Tirumaraiyur, South India (C. S. I.) founded.

1951 Representatives of eight denominations and two independent groups meet at Cincinnati to give consideration to a plan of union for a proposed "United Church of Christ."

1951 Federation of the Hungarian, Slovak, Croatian, and Slovenian Lutheran groups in Yugoslavia formed.

1951 Covenant of co-operation between the Congregational Union of England and Wales and the Assembly of the Presbyterian Church in England signed in London.

1951 European Laymen's Conference at Bad Boll, Germany.

*1951 Evangelical Lutheran Church formed in the U. S. from two bodies.

*1951 Reunion of the Evangelical Lutheran Church and the Restored Evangelical Lutheran Church completed in Amsterdam, Holland.

†1952 Delegates from the Church of India, Pakistan, Burma, and Ceylon (Anglican), the Methodist Church of Southern Asia, the British Methodist Churches, the North India Baptists, and the United Church of Northern India and Pakistan (Presbyterian and Congregationalist) agree on a tentative plan for forming a United Church of North India. Disciples and United Presbyterians "observe" sessions.

*1952 The Evangelical Church of Thuringia formed from many small regional churches in the area.

1952 Opening of the Graduate School of Ecumenical Studies. Chateau de Bossey, Celigny. Sponsored by World Council of Church's Ecumenical Institute and associated with the University of Geneva.

1952 The General Assemblies of the Presbyterian Church U.S.A., the Presbyterian Church U.S., and the United Presbyterian Church approve negotiations toward eventual merger.

1952 The Evangelical Lutheran Church, the United Evangelical Lutheran Church, and the American Lutheran Church vote to continue plans for merger. The Lutheran Free Church votes to continue participation in merger negotiations but is not now ready for organic merger. The Augustana Lutheran Church formally withdraws from the plan.

1952 The Riverside Church and the Judson Memorial Church (both Baptist) were accepted as members of the New York Congregational Church Association.

1952 A Canadian Lutheran Council established (United Lutheran Church in America, Evangelical Lutheran Church, American Lutheran Church, Augustana Lutheran Church, United Evangelical Lutheran Church and Lutheran Free Church).

*1952 Evangelical Presbyterian Church of Portugal formed by 12 communities in Portugal and the Azores.

*1952 The Fellowship of Independent Baptist Churches in Canada unanimously approves a merger with the Union of Regular Baptist Churches of Ontario and Quebec.

1952 World Conference on Faith and Order. Lund.

†1952 Meeting of the International Missionary Council. Willingen.

1953 The Italian Methodist Synod meets in February and passes a resolution to resume discussions with the Waldensian Church on union between the two churches.

1953 Representatives of the Evangelical Lutheran Church, American Lutheran Church, United Evangelical Lutheran Church, and Lutheran Free Church meet in Joint Union Committee to complete plan for merger.

†1953 International Christian University in Japan opens.

1953 Representatives of the Presbyterian Church U.S.A., the Presbyterian Church U.S., and the United Presbyterian Church approve a revised plan of union.

†1953 A new united theological school founded at Makassar, Celebes, with contributions from The Methodist Church, Presbyterian U.S.A., United Presbyterian and Reformed Churches, and the Dutch Reformed Church.

*1953 The Evangelical Mennonite Brethren and the Evangelical Mennonite Church unite to form the Conference of Evangelical Mennonites.

1953 Congress de Jerunesse Orthodoxe meets at Sèvres, France, in April.

†1953 A plan for Church Union in North India completed and submitted to the participating denominations.

†1953 Council of Churches on a Lutheran Basis in Southwest Africa established in Pretoria.

†1953 United Presbyterian Seminary at Gujranwala, West Pakistan, established.

1954 Ecumenical Council of the Churches of Denmark established.

†1954 A plan for the union of five church groups in Northern India and Pakistan completed by the Negotiating Committee and sent to the governing bodies of the communions involved.

†1954 The Mar Thoma Church approves immediate intercommunion with the Church of South India.

1954 The Second Assembly of the World Council of Churches. Evanston, Illinois.

†1954 The Southern Rhodesia Christian Conference formed.

1954 The Welsh Ecumenical Society inaugurated.

1954 An Ecumenical Council of Czech Churches formed.

*1955 Merger of the Philadelphia Yearly Meeting of Friends and the Yearly Meeting of the Religious Society of Friends of Philadelphia and Vicinity forming the Philadelphia Yearly Meeting and the Religious Society of Friends.

†1955 Formation of the Ecumenical Society of Jamaica.

†1955 Hong Kong: Delegates from Asian churches and mission boards (Japan, Korea, Formosa, Hong Kong, Philippines, Malaya, Thailand, and Indonesia) establish the Asia Council on Ecumenical Mission.

1955 First biennial convention of the Council of Liberal Churches (Universalist and Unitarian) in Detroit. The Council votes to poll their congregations and devise a merger plan.

†1955 First All-African Lutheran Conference. Marangu, Tanganyika.

†1955 Conference on the Responsible Society. São Paulo, Brazil.

*1956 The union of the Presbyterian Church of East Africa and the Church of Scotland Overseas Presbytery of Kenya form an autonomous united Presbyterian Church of East Africa.

§1956 The Moravian Church of the Brethren (of Ladakh) join the United Church of North India.

†1956 First Congress of Evangelical Churches (Associate Reformed Presbyterian, Disciples of Christ, and Congregational) in Guadalajara.

§1956 The United Church in North Australia formed by the merger of the Methodist, Congregational, and the Presbyterian Churches in Australia's Northern Territory.

1956 Intercommunion achieved between the Evangelical Lutheran Church in the Netherlands and the Reformed Church of the Netherlands.

§†1956 The Tagalog Disciples convention vote in favor of union with the United Church of the Philippines.

*1956 The Original Secession Church (seceded in 1733) returns to the Church of Scotland.

1956 Members of the Church of England and the Church of Scotland admitted to Holy Communion in the Church of Denmark.

*1956 The United Church of South Africa (Congregational) formed from the Congregational Churches of the London Missionary Society, the American Board, and the Congregational Union of South Africa.

†1957 Union of Chosen Christian University and Severance Union Medical College, forming Yonsei University in Korea.

†1957 Organization of the Argentine Federation of Churches.

1957 The Presbyterian Church, The Methodist Church, the Congregational Churches, and the Associated Churches of Christ in New Zealand vote in favor of merger, provided a plan of union can be agreed upon.

†1957 Organization of the Federación Uruguay de Iglesias Evangélicas.

†1957 Organization of Kerala Christian Council. State of Kerala, India.

†1957 East Asia Christian Conference, Prapat, Indonesia, votes to establish a regional ecumenical organization.

§†1957 Union of the Presbyterian U.S.A., missions of Western India, Punjab, and North India and the United Church of Northern India.

1957 Conference of European Churches founded in Liselund, Denmark.

§1957 The Uniting General Synod of the Congregational Christian Churches and the Evangelical and Reformed Church form the United Church of Christ. Cleveland, Ohio.

†1957 Ratification of the constitution of St. Paul's United Theological College (Anglican, Methodist, and Presbyterian). Limuru, Kenya.

1957 North American Conference on Faith and Order. Oberlin, Ohio.

†1957–58 I.M.C. Assembly. University College, Ghana.

†1958 All-Africa Church Conference. Ibadan, Nigeria.

1958 Four Natal younger churches vote to negotiate merger: Mankankanana Lutheran, Evangelical Lutheran Zulu, Norwegian Lutheran Zulu, and Zulu-Swazi Synod.

*1958 The Free Methodist Church of North America approves merger with the Holiness Movement Church in Canada.

*†1958 The Orthodox Syrian Church of Malabar and the Malankara Jacobite Syrian Church reconciled.

*1958 Union of the United Presbyterian Church of North America and the Presbyterian Church U.S.A., to form The United Presbyterian Church U.S.A.

*1958 The Danish Baptist General Council of America (1956) disbands, and its churches join the American Baptist Convention.

1959 Methodist Church in Austria, Lutherans of the Augsburg Confession, and Evangelical Reformed Church (Heidelberg Conference) join in a National Council of Churches in Austria.

†1959 Inaugural Assembly of the East Asia Christian Conference at Kuala Lumpur, Malaya.

1959 Constituting Assembly of the National Student Christian Federation, U.S.A., at Oberlin College.

†1959 Major steps toward unification taken by the Presbyterian Church of the Cameroons and the African Protestant Church.

1960 The Augustana Lutheran Church, the Finnish Evangelical

       Lutheran Church, the American Evangelical Lutheran Church, and the United Lutheran Church in America vote to form the Lutheran Church in America.

*1960 The Evangelical Lutheran Church, the American Lutheran Church, and the United Evangelical Lutheran Church merge to form The American Lutheran Church.

*1960 Three Canadian Lutheran groups merge to form the Evangelical Lutheran Church of Canada.

*†1960 Four Natal Lutheran bodies join to form a single Evangelical Lutheran Church of Zulu-Xhosa-Swazi Region (see 1958).

*1960 The American Unitarian Association and the Universalist Church of America vote to form the Unitarian Universalist Association.

  1960 First National Conference of Australian Churches, Melbourne, February 2–11.

  1960 Australian Council for the World Council of Churches changes its name to the Australian Council of Churches.

  1960 First European Ecumenical Youth Assembly, Lausanne, July 13–24, 1960.

APPENDIX II

*A DRAFT PLAN FOR THE INTEGRATION OF THE WORLD COUNCIL OF CHURCHES and THE INTERNATIONAL MISSIONARY COUNCIL**

I. INTRODUCTION

A

The question is asked: Why should two world bodies, the International Missionary Council and the World Council of Churches, become integrated into a single organism? The answer is this. A basic and long-forgotten truth is being rediscovered in our time, which might be stated thus: the *unity* of the Church and the *mission* of the Church both belong, in equal degree, to the *essence* of the Church. If Christian churches would be in very truth the Church, they must carry the Gospel into all the world. They must also strive to achieve the unity of all those throughout the world for whom Jesus Christ is Lord. This truth has already become manifest in the life of both the world bodies. It has led them into association with each other and now obliges them to go farther. They exist to help the churches to witness to the wholeness of the Gospel and must, therefore, seek to express that wholeness in their own life.

B

These two world bodies have, under God, been brought into being through specific historical events. In this process, they are now drawing more closely together as organs of what has come to be called the Ecumenical Movement.

The World Missionary Conference, held in Edinburgh in 1910, was the source from which a world movement for missionary co-operation took its rise. This led to the formation of the International Missionary Council in 1921.

From the same source the churches derived a fresh impetus towards unity, and a deepened concern for the Christian witness to men in

---

* Report of the Joint Committee to the International Missionary Council and the World Council of Churches, 1957. The Plan as submitted by the two world bodies to their constituent councils and churches omits sections "I. INTRODUCTION" and "II. THE PLAN." Modifications in the details of the Plan as adopted in 1958, 1959, and 1960 have been incorporated in the text.

society. The fresh impetus toward unity found expression in the *Faith and Order* movement. The deepened concern for the Christian witness to men in society was reflected in the parallel movement known as *Life and Work*.

The first formal steps to bring these two movements together in a World Council of Churches were taken in 1938, and in the war years that followed the Council operated "in the process of formation." In 1948, the World Council of Churches was inaugurated at Amsterdam.

Even prior to this, in 1946, the World Council of Churches "in process of formation" and in the International Missionary Council joined in the creation of the Commission of the Churches on International Affairs. At the time of the Amsterdam Assembly they decided to operate "in association." In 1949, the W.C.C. and the I.M.C. agreed to establish a Joint Secretariat for East Asia. In 1952, the I.M.C. requested the W.C.C. to permit its Division of Interchurch Aid and Service to Refugees to act on behalf of both bodies in administering emergency interchurch aid and relief in countries outside Europe. In 1954, the growing importance of the work of the Joint Committee was recognized by the appointment of a full-time Secretary. In the same year the Research Secretariat of the I.M.C. was combined with the Study Department of the W.C.C. in a joint Division of Studies, with a Department of Missionary Studies as an integral part of the Division. In these and other ways the "association" of the two Councils has become increasingly interlocked and more visibly interdependent.

C

During this period, churches of Asia, Africa, and Latin America have played an increasing part in all the concerns of the Ecumenical Movement. Many of these churches are now related to both the world bodies. Both make claims on their leadership.

A still more significant point should be noted. Pressure for the integration of the I.M.C. and the W.C.C. has come with growing insistence from churches and councils that desire to be related to a single organization concerned with both the mission and the unity of the Church. The proposed formation of the East Asia Christian Conference marks a new era in this process. All this points to a relationship that goes beyond "association."

This continuous development expresses a logic inherent in the present ecumenical situation, which led the Joint Committee at its meeting in 1956

to recommend to the parent bodies that in the opinion of the Joint Committee the time has come when consideration should be given to the possibility of full integration between the W.C.C. and the I.M.C., subject to an adequate safeguarding in any plan of integra-

tion of the distinctive expression of the Mission of the Church, as this
has been embodied in the I.M.C.

In making this decision the leaders of the two world bodies were concerned with far more than efficiency of organization. As the document
on "The Calling of the Church to Mission and to Unity" (adopted by
the Central Committee of the W.C.C. in 1951) pointed out: "The missionary movement has been from the beginning imbued with a deep
sense of the calling to unity. . . . The movement toward unity has from
the beginning concerned itself with the Church's witness to the world."
The main concern of the two Councils must be the total task of the
Church in the world. That task includes both the witness of the Church
to the ends of the earth and the concern for the manifestation of the
unity of the Body of Christ.

The Joint Committee has, therefore, laid down the following requirements for an acceptable plan of integration: "The Committee
regards it as imperative that any such integration should be in a form
which ensures that missions belong to the heart of the ecumenical
movement. It should also be on lines which bring the missionary forces
into closer relationship with all phases of the Church's witness in the life
of the world."

D

Any plan to integrate the International Missionary Council and the
World Council of Churches must recognize, and at the same time make
clear to all the churches and councils concerned, some very important
facts.

First: The emergence of a dynamic regionalism in the world of our
time—the feeling of peoples in great areas of the globe that they belong
together and are involved in a common destiny—is a factor of great
significance. Churches and councils in different regions are in different
stages of development and have differing perspectives with regard to
the ecumenical ideal. The needs and developments within the regions
themselves must determine the pattern of the ecumenical service given
and received. The plan of integration here presented seeks to provide
an organization that will be sensitive and flexible enough to respond
to the developing regional situations.

Second: The proposals that follow are concerned with integration
only at the international level. They do not determine or prejudge the
form of organization within National Christian Councils or between
churches and missionary bodies. The integrated Council and its Commission will have no constitutional authority over their member bodies.

Third: It is to be noted that the plan provides for (*a*) national or
regional Christian Councils to be formally associated with the integrated
Council; (*b*) national or regional Christian or Missionary Councils to
be affiliated only with the commission; (*c*) freedom of councils to have

either relationship separately or both together.

Fourth: No plan can by itself ensure the spiritual integration that is our deepest desire. This can come only as the gift of God. Nevertheless, this plan is submitted to the two world bodies, in the conviction that its realization will represent a decisive step of obedience toward the fulfillment of the total task that the Lord has entrusted to the whole Church.

II. THE PLAN

It is proposed that the integration of the World Council of Churches and the International Missionary Council be effected by the following actions:

A. *The carrying forward and extension of the work of the I.M.C. by*
  (1) *The creation of a Commission on World Mission and Evangelism of the W.C.C.* as described below, to which the existing member councils of the I.M.C. will be affiliated;
  (2) *The creation of a Division of World Mission and Evangelism* comparable to the divisional units within the present W.C.C.;
  (3) *Representation of those with missionary knowledge and experience* in the Assembly, Central, and Executive Committees of the integrated Council;
  (4) *Provision for such continuous assistance to the work of national and regional councils* as may be desired, and attention to their participation in the work of the integrated Council.

B. *Changes in the Constitution of the W.C.C.,* including
  (1) The revision of the functions of the W.C.C. (Constitution, Sec. III) as follows:
      (i) To carry on the work of the world movements for Faith and Order and Life and Work, and the work of the *International Missionary Council;*
      (ii) To facilitate common action by the churches;
      (iii) To promote co-operation in study;
      (iv) To promote the growth of ecumenical and *missionary* consciousness in the members of all churches;
      (v) To establish and maintain relations with other ecumenical movements, with denominational federations of world-wide scope *and with national and regional councils;*
      (vi) To call world conferences on specific subjects as occasion may require, such conferences being empowered to publish their own findings;
      (vii) To support the churches in their *world-wide* missionary and evangelistic task.
  (2) Changes in Sec. VI to provide for the Commission on World Mission and Evangelism.
  (3) Such consequential changes as will provide for A(3) and A(4)

above and other steps necessary to take care of I.M.C. responsibilities.

C. *Re-examination and adaptation of the present work of the W.C.C.* with a view to relating all the activities of the council to the missionary task and concern of the churches.

The following sections indicate more fully the detailed steps proposed.

PROPOSED CONSTITUTION OF THE COMMISSION ON WORLD MISSION AND EVANGELISM AND THE DIVISION OF WORLD MISSION AND EVANGELISM

THE COMMISSION ON WORLD MISSION AND EVANGELISM

1. There shall be a Commission on World Mission and Evangelism constituted in accordance with the Constitution of the World Council of Churches (Sec. VI, (3)).

2. *Aim*
   Its aim shall be to further the proclamation to the whole world of the Gospel of Jesus Christ, to the end that all men may believe in him and be saved.

3. *Functions*
   The functions of the Commission shall be:
   - (i) To keep before the churches their calling and privilege to engage in constant prayer for the missionary and evangelistic work of the Church;
   - (ii) To remind the churches of the range and character of the unfinished evangelistic task and to deepen their sense of missionary obligation;
   - (iii) To stimulate thought and study on the Biblical and theological bases and meaning of the Church's missionary task and on questions directly related to the spread of the Gospel in the world;
   - (iv) To foster among churches and among councils and other Christian bodies more effective co-operation and united action for world evangelization;
   - (v) To deepen evangelistic and missionary concern in the whole life and work of the World Council of Churches;
   - (vi) To assist in securing and safeguarding freedom of conscience and religion as formulated in declarations of the World Council of Churches on religious liberty;
   - (vii) To co-operate with other units of the World Council of Churches;

(viii) To take such further action in fulfillment of the declared aim of the Commission as is not otherwise provided for within the World Council of Churches.

4. *Authority*

The Commission shall have no mandatory authority over any of the councils related to it, whether in affiliated or consultative relationship, in accordance with the principles enunciated in the Constitution of the World Council of Churches.

5. *Operations*

(i) The Commission shall ordinarily meet once every five years. Special meetings may be convened at the call of the Divisional Committee with the approval of the Central Committee.

(ii) The Commission shall formulate the general lines of policy and program to be followed by the Division of World Mission and Evangelism, for submission to the Central Committee for its approval. The Division shall be responsible for the execution of this policy and program.

(iii) The Commission shall keep its related councils fully informed and consult them regularly on matters of policy and program. It shall send its reports and recommendations to the councils.

(iv) The Commission shall report regularly to the Assembly and the Central Committee.

(v) The Commission shall develop appropriate organs for fulfilling its functions in the area of evangelism, including the provision of staff for this purpose.

(vi)

(a) The Commission may sponsor—or, with the approval of the Assembly or Central Committee, co-operate with other bodies in sponsoring—agencies for specialized activities.

(b) In each case of a sponsored agency, the Constitution and the appointment of the principal executive officer shall be subject to the approval of the Commission. Each sponsored agency shall report to the Commission from time to time on its acts and program.

(c) The World Council shall not be responsible for the financing of sponsored agencies except as it may in advance explicitly accept such responsibility.

6. *Affiliation and Membership*

(i) All member councils of the International Missionary Council at the time of integration will be regarded as affiliated to the Commission.

(ii) Thereafter national or regional Christian councils and national or regional missionary organizations that accept the aim of the Commission may become councils affiliated to the Commission, on the approval of a regularly constituted meeting of the Commission by a two-thirds majority of those present and voting. Any application for affiliation between meetings of the Commission may be considered by the Divisional Committee; if the application is supported by a two-thirds majority of the members of the Committee present and voting, this action shall be communicated to the councils affiliated to the Commission, and unless objection is received from more than one third of these councils within six months, the council shall be declared affiliated.

The following criteria shall determine eligibility for affiliation:

(a) The council shall express its acceptance of the aim of the Commission on World Mission and Evangelism and desire to co-operate in the functions of the Commission as defined in the Constitution.

(b) The council shall satisfy such other criteria as may be determined by the Commission. In considering applications for affiliation, the Commission on World Mission and Evangelism will take into account the size and stability of the council concerned and the relevance of its program to the aim and functions of the Commission.

(c) There shall be consultation with the member churches of the World Council of Churches in the area concerned, and with the Committee on National Council Relationships.

(iii) A council that performs functions in several fields of activity may be represented in the Commission on World Mission and Evangelism through its appropriate unit(s) or division(s).

(iv) National or regional Christian councils and national or regional missionary organizations that are not affiliated to the Commission may become councils in consultation with the Commission. If any member council of the International Missionary Council informs the International Missionary Council before integration that it cannot accept affiliation, it shall automatically become a council in consultation with the Commission under this rule. Thereafter, councils in consultation shall be councils which are not yet eligible to become affiliated councils or which do not desire affiliation, but which

(a) accept the aim of the Commission and desire a consultative relationship with it; and

(b) are accepted by the Commission as eligible for such a

relationship. Councils in consultation shall be entitled to send consultants to meetings of the Commission: they shall be entitled to speak but not to vote.

(v) In accordance with a schedule that shall be prepared before each regular meeting of the Commission by the Divisional Committee and approved by the Central Committee, the Commission shall consist of members appointed by the affiliated councils and of members appointed by the Central Committee. The members appointed by Central Committee shall include persons representative of the field of evangelism. Their number shall not exceed one half of the number of places allotted to affiliated councils.

(For the first meeting of the Commission eighty members shall be appointed by affiliated councils; thirty-five shall be appointed by the Central Committee, fifteen of whom shall represent the work of evangelism.)

(vi) In addition to the consultants representing councils in consultation, the Divisional Committee may provide for the attendance at meetings of the Commission of persons with special competence in the field of missions as advisers. They shall be entitled to speak but not to vote.

(For the first meeting of the Commission, advisers shall not exceed fifteen in number and shall be appointed by the Administrative Committee of the International Missionary Council.)

(vii) Each sponsored agency may appoint a representative to attend the meetings of the Commission and of the Divisional Committee. They shall be entitled to speak but not to vote.

(viii) The Divisional Committee may also invite observers to meetings of the Commission from councils and other missionary agencies that are not related to the Commission. Observers will be entitled to speak but not to vote.

(ix) The members of the Commission shall serve until appointments have been made for the next meeting of the Commission or until their successors are appointed.

(x) An affiliated council may withdraw from the Commission, but must give at least one year's written notice to the next regularly constituted meeting of the Commission or of the Divisional Committee; withdrawal shall become effective at the close of that meeting.

7. *Officers and Secretariat*

(i) At each regular meeting the Commission shall appoint a a Chairman and one or more Vice-Chairmen whose term of office shall extend from the beginning of that meeting to the beginning of the next regular meeting. The nomination of the Chairman and Vice-Chairmen shall be made by the Divisional Committee prior to the meeting of the Commission.

(ii) The same Secretariat shall serve both the Commission and the Division.

(iii) The Commission may appoint an Honorary Treasurer or Treasurers.

8. *Finance*

(i) The Commission in consultation with its affiliated and other supporting councils shall prepare a budget for submission to the Central Committee for its approval.

(ii) The Commission shall be responsible for the raising and expenditure of funds in accordance with the approved budget.

(iii) The funds formerly vested in the International Missionary Council for general or specific purposes, together with such additional funds as may from time to time be entrusted to the Commission for the discharge of its functions, shall be vested in the World Council of Churches. Such funds shall be used solely for the purposes of the Commission and, if designated, in accordance with the wishes of the donor or testator. These funds shall be administered by the Commission, subject to the approval of the Central Committee.

(iv) The Commission shall provide for the cost of its staff and offices, of the meetings of the Commission and the Division and its committees, of all operations authorized by the Commission and of all services provided for the Commission by the World Council of Churches.

(v) In their financial operations the Commission and Division shall follow the procedures prescribed in the Bylaws.

9. *Quorum*

One third of the members of the Commission shall constitute a quorum at any given session, provided that those present at the session come from at least three continents and represent at least one third of the affiliated councils.

10. *Bylaws*

The Commission may make, amend, and repeal bylaws for the conduct of the business of the Commission.

11. *Revision*

The Constitution of the Commission and of the Division may be amended, subject to the approval of Central Committee, by a two-thirds majority of the Commission, provided the proposed amendment shall have been reviewed by the Divisional Committee and notice of it sent to the affiliated councils not less than six months before the meeting of the Commission. The Divisional Committee as well as the affiliated councils shall have the right to propose amendments.

THE DIVISION OF WORLD MISSION AND EVANGELISM

1. The Division of World Mission and Evangelism shall consist of the Divisional Committee and staff.

2. *Function*
   The Division of World Mission and Evangelism shall be responsible for carrying out the aim and functions of the Commission on World Mission and Evangelism and shall act for it between its meetings save in such matters as the Commission may have reserved to its own authority.

3. *Activities*
   The activities of the Division shall include:
   (i) Aiding the churches in their missionary and evangelistic task and where requested by churches or councils acting on their behalf.
   (ii) Maintaining relationships of mutual helpfulness with councils affiliated to and in consultation with the Commission and with member churches of the World Council of Churches concerning the work of the Commission and Division.
   (iii) Fostering relationships with other councils.
   (iv) Publishing such literature as may be called for in the furtherance of the aim and functions of the Commission.
   (v) Convening such conferences as may be required.
   (vi) Responsibility for any departments that may be created within the Division, and guiding their work.
   (vii) Co-operating with the other divisions of the World Council to carry out the purposes and functions of the Commission and of the World Council effectively.
   (viii) Responsibility for the raising and administration of the funds of the Commission in accordance with clause 8 (ii) of the Constitution of the Commission.

4. *The Divisional Committee*

(i) There shall be a Divisional Committee responsible for the general conduct of the work of the Division, which shall report to the Assembly and to the Central Committee as well as to the Commission. It will also report to its related councils.

(ii) The Committee shall consist of not less than twenty or more than twenty-five members, appointed annually by the Central Committee on the nomination of the Commission or, in the absence of a meeting of the Commission, of the Divisional Committee. The Chairman and one member of each departmental committee within the Division shall be included in the membership of the Central Committee. The membership of the Committee shall be as representative as possible, geographically and confessionally and of men and women. The Chairman and Vice-Chairmen of the Commission shall be ex officio members of the Divisional Committee.

(iii) The Divisional Committee shall ordinarily meet once a year. Special meetings may be called on the authority of the officers.

(iv) The Committee shall prepare, through such procedures as the Commission may determine, an annual budget, which shall be submitted in advance of the beginning of each year to the Finance Committee of the Central Committee, which shall forward it to the Central Committee with any comments it may wish to make. The Committee shall submit financial reports to each meeting of the Finance Committee of the Central Committee.

(v) The Divisional Committee shall nominate its Chairman for appointment by the Central Committee.

(vi) The Director of the Division shall be nominated by the Divisional Committee in consultation with the staffing committee of the Executive Committee and shall be appointed by the Central Committee as an Associate General Secretary of the World Council and Director of the Division. The Divisional Committee shall determine, subject to the approval of the Central Committee, the number of the staff of the Commission and the Division. The Secretaries shall be appointed according to the Rules of the World Council, on the nomination of the Divisional Committee.

(vii) The Divisional Committee shall determine the principal duties of the staff of the Commission and the Division.

(viii) One half of the membership of the Divisional Committee shall constitute a quorum at any ordinary meeting, provided that those present come from at least three continents and five affiliated councils.

INDEX

INDEX

Advent Christian Church, 65
Adventist churches, 63 ff.
"Affiliated councils" of the W.C.C.,
145
Africa, 30 f., 77 ff., 95 f.
Africa Evangelistic Band, 64
Africa Inland Mission, 64
Africa south of the Sahara mission, 27
Algeria Evangelical Missionary Council, 41
All-Africa Church Conference, 66
Allen, Yorke, 67 f.
American Bible Society, 36, 103, 110
American Board of Commissioners
for Foreign Missions, 33, 36 f., 103,
121
American theology, 80 ff.
Amsterdam Assembly of the W.C.C.
(1948), 97, 123, 127, 138
Anglicanism, 24 n. 4, 31, 70, 85, 89
Angola Evangelical Alliance, 41
Annual Conference of the Foreign
Mission Boards, 26
Aquinas, 79
Aristotelianism, 74, 78
Assemblies of God, 64 f.
"Associated councils" of the W.C.C.,
139, 142, 145
Athanasius, 77
Augustine, 77, 78
Australian Council of the W.C.C.,
41
Austria Ecumenical Council of
Churches, 41
Authority of the Faith, The, 74 n. 16
Azariah, Bishop, 30
Bangkok conference, 1949, 138
Baptism, 86
Baptist Missionary Society, 25, 28
Baptists, 86
Barnes, Roswell P., 104
Barth, Karl, 80

Basel Evangelical Missionary Society,
36
"Basis" of the W.C.C., 150
Belgian Federation of the Protestant
Churches, 40
"Believer's baptism," 86
Bennett, John C., 104, 108 n. 5
Berean African Missionary Society, 64
Bethesda Bolivian Mission, 64
Bible, 77
Bible and Medical Missionary Fellowship, 37 n. 24
Bible schools, 58, 69
Bible societies, 36, 42, 59, 133
Bilheimer, Robert S., 15 n. 7
Blake, Eugene Carson, 108 n. 5
Board for Christian Work in Santo
Domingo, 134
"Body of Christ," 14, 62, 126
Bolivia United Evangelical Churches,
41, 64
Bombay Missionary Union, 27
Book of Common Prayer, The, 78
Boyer, Père, 15 n. 6
Brazil Evangelical Federation, 40
Brent, Charles H., 131
British and Foreign Bible Society, 36,
103, 110
British Council of Churches, 41
Brown, William Adams, 103, 104, 137
Brown, William Adams, Ecumenical
Library, 10, 59, Appendix I
Burma Christian Council, 41
Cairo Conference (1906), 31
"Calling of the Church to Mission
and to Unity, The," 140
Cameroons and Equatorial Evangelical Federation, 41
Canadian Council of Churches, 41
Canterbury Societies, 121
Carey, William, 28 f.
Cavert, Samuel McCrea, 96, 104

199